The Ministry in Transition

A Case Study of Theological Education

Yoshio Fukuyama

The Pennsylvania State University Press
University Park and London

Library of Congress Catalog Card Number 72–1395
International Standard Book Number 0–271–01129–7

Printed in the United States of America
Designed by Madge McKinley

Library of Congress Cataloging in Publication Data
Fukuyama, Yoshio, 1921–
The ministry in transition.

Includes bibliographical references.
1. United Church of Christ—Clergy, Training of.
2. Theology—Study and teaching—United States.
I. Title.
BX9884.A3F83 207'.11'5834 72–1395
ISBN O–271–001129–7

The Ministry in Transition

A Case Study of Theological Education

To Truman Bartlett Douglass

1901–1969

Contents

Foreword

There are personal reasons for my writing these lines with particular pleasure. Few associations, if any, have meant more to me and my wife than our formal and informal relationships, dating back to the 1950s, with the Board for Homeland Ministries of the (now) United Church of Christ. The Fukuyamas and the Napiers, though rarely together in recent years, have long been bound by ties of affection. It would be impossible for me to give expression to the kind of indebtedness we feel to Truman Douglass, to whom this book is dedicated; to Wesley Hotchkiss, whose steady support of the work is acknowledged by the author; and to the present leadership of the Board, especially the Howard Spraggs, whom we first came to know in those marvelous summers of the Pastors' School in Deering, New Hampshire.

And there are, of course, professional reasons for my writing this Foreword. This is a significant and uniquely informative study of theological education which comes to all of us who care about the church precisely in a time when our need of light and direction is most critical. For the sake of all of us in church and seminary, I hope to see the widest possible circulation and the most intensive reading and discussion of the study. I shall see to it that the members of my own faculty have it. And I shall recommend it among the churches. As Dr. Fukuyama says (and it is a point which he reiterates in different ways), "The problem of the minister's vocation is nothing more than the problem of the church in today's world."

In reading and using and discussing this book, we will not miss the importance of the phrase "in today's world." A couple of years ago James Reston of the New York Times, reviewing the decade of the 1960s wrote: "It would be a foolish man who denied the plain facts. We are overpopulated, undercivilized, divided, corrupted, and bewildered, 'destitute of faith and terrified of skepticism.' War, crime, pollution, racial tension, political cynicism and pessimism are our companions." In the same column he quoted Whitehead's comment (written in the 1920s), which some of us in seminary and church may sometimes suspect to be sharply applicable to us. We must recognize, Whitehead said, "that the major advances in civilization are processes which all but wreck the society in which they occur."

Running throughout this vital study is evidence of the strains imposed upon the people and institutions of theology by the multiple crises of anguish that plague the human family. In seminary and church it takes the form of extreme tension between the two historical, legitimate, essential functions of the community of faith, those of coping and changing, or, in Dr. Fukuyama's terms, comforting and challenging. Let the reader read with sensitivity to the critical needs for both.

As you will presently see, the primary objective of the book is "to provide empirical grounds for the current discussions about the purpose of the church and its ministry." It is an exhaustive look at the feelings and opinions and judgments of 1,191 pastors of the United Church of Christ and 1,283 students in United Church of Christ and related seminaries. Some of the results reported in the study are surprising, at least to me:

1. Preoccupation with concerns of personal identity and commitment ranks considerably lower on the scale than I would have thought, both among pastors and seminarians.
2. Fifty-seven per cent of the responding pastors and 44 per cent of the seminarians are strongly or moderately supportive of the viability of the parish church. In re-

cent years some of us would have thought that disillusionment with the church might have returned lower percentages, although all of us are aware of and welcome a marked change in the direction of increased affirmation.

3. Seventy-five per cent of the students coming into the independent seminaries (which have always tended to draw a higher proportion of the dissident and/or the unchurched) come from active or very active roles of leadership in the church.
4. The study suggests that strengthened departments of religion in colleges and universities are producing more seminarians more deeply motivated by theological and ethical concerns than by an "existential or empirical response to objective social conditions."
5. Of all the courses listed among the 13 seminaries, the field of history of religions accounts for only 3.44 per cent and that of contemporary culture only 2.53. All the rest are in the traditional disciplines (including the now well-established field of religion and personality, accounting for 6.42 per cent). "Where would you put your emphasis in further study?" Forty per cent of the ministers and 32 per cent of the students named psychology.

Some results confirm what we have suspected:

1. A majority of all respondents had been undergraduates in denominational schools. Municipal and community colleges, for good or ill, send virtually none of their graduates into theology.
2. Interdenominational, independent, university-related theological schools attract a higher proportion of collegiate honor students.
3. A large majority of all respondents are dissatisfied with their own seminary's sense of community.
4. The seminary has a liberalizing effect on the theological and social views of the student.

5. Pulpit and pew are widely separated on social views, social problems (but not, the study finds, "on collision course," as some would put it). There is a real gap in the understanding of the purpose of the church and its ministry.

And surprising or not, depending upon the reader, there is a vast and pervasive disaffection with the total performance of the seminaries. Only 11 per cent of the ministers and 6 per cent (!) of the seminarians felt that "on the whole, theological education is doing a good job training ministers." In other words, a fourth of the pastors and a third of the students believe that seminary education in the United States "needs to be completely overhauled."

Change, even radical change in the sense simply of change at the roots, is of course occurring in these same and other seminaries. The study is based upon data acquired in 1967. One suspects that in some particulars we in the seminaries would fare better now precisely because we have already been responding to conditions laid empirically before us in the study.

But we have miles to go; with no sign of let-up in the frightful pace of change in which we are all caught up, we will continue to have miles to go. *The Ministry in Transition* is a gift to all of us in church and seminary, a gift that will help us find our way.

DAVIE NAPIER

President
Pacific School of Religion
Berkeley, California

Preface

This case study of theological education in America describes how a major Protestant denomination recruits and trains its clergy. As a social study, it gives empirical content to one denomination's understanding of the purpose of the church and its ministry.

The investigation reported in this volume had its origin in a resolution passed in 1965 by the General Synod of the United Church of Christ asking its Board for Homeland Ministries to organize a Study Commission on Theological Education and to deal "with the whole problem of the most effective way of training our ministers and of financing that training."

A more candid reason for the establishment of the Study Commission was given by Dr. Truman B. Douglass, then the chief executive officer of the United Church Board for Homeland Ministries. He addressed the initial meeting of the Study Commission with these words:

> We need to remember the initial motivation for this study. In a sense, it was a consequence of economic determinism. The issue arose because of an obvious need, that of more adequate support for theological education in the United Church of Christ. We are caught in a whirlpool of conflicting ideas about theological education and the mission of the church. There is insufficient clarity about our direction. We probably have more seminaries than the United Church of Christ could support. The problem is to find the criteria for judgment as to where the limited strength of the denomination should be focused. The study indicates that very few changes have occurred in the shape of theological education since Aquinas and that our tardiness of adaptation to social change is

> demonstrated by vast changes in other professions such as law and medicine. These suspicions generated our study.[1]

Economic stringencies have a way of forcing institutions to reexamine their goals and to reorganize their priorities. For the United Church of Christ another important factor was at work. The union which formed the denomination in 1957 brought two divergent traditions together. The Evangelical and Reformed Church was rooted in the tradition of German pietism and the Swiss reformation; the Congregational Christian Churches traced their origins to England and the Calvinist theological tradition. In polity, the former was presbyterian, the latter congregational. Evangelical and Reformed congregations were most numerous in Pennsylvania and Missouri, while Congregationalists were identified with New England since colonial times.

Given such diversity, it became inevitable for the United Church of Christ to face squarely the problem of theological education in terms that transcended the immediate fiscal crisis. Dr. Douglass made this point clear when he told the Commission, "We are caught in a whirlpool of conflicting ideas about theological education and the mission of the church." The fundamental purpose of the Study Commission on Theological Education was to clarify the mission of the church; the study of its theological schools provided the opportunity to pursue questions relating to the church's mission and its ministry in a systematic and empirical way.

The Study Commission was fortunate enough to secure the services of Professor Paul M. Harrison of The Pennsylvania State University to direct the study during the academic year 1966–1967. Dr. Harrison's credentials for this assignment were well known to members of the Commission. His case study of the American Baptist Convention, reported in the volume *Authority and Power in the Free Church Tradition,* has become a classic monograph in the sociology of religion.[2] As an American Baptist clergyman, he brought to his work his profound understanding of the nature and mission of the church as well as his knowledge and skill as a social scientist and academician. His findings were presented to the Commission in his report, "Theological Education and the United Church of Christ," in the spring of 1967.

It was my good fortune to work closely with Professor Harrison in his research. At that time I was the Secretary for Research of the United Church Board for Homeland Ministries. Since then I have joined him on the faculty of the Department of Religious Studies at The Pennsylvania State University.

As Professor Harrison's research for the Study Commission was drawing to a close, we decided to use the occasion to conduct a survey of those recently ordained in the denomination and of students enrolled in the seminaries. Having in mind the kinds of problems and issues explored by him through interviews, participant observation, and the analyses of seminary publications, we developed a questionnaire to test some of his findings and to explore other issues.

Since our focus was on theological education, we decided to include all persons ordained during the preceding five-year period (1962–1966) and a sampling of those ordained during the previous decade (1952–1961). We also included all students enrolled in the thirteen theological schools affiliated with the United Church of Christ during the academic year 1966–1967 in our survey population.

The design and method used in this study are briefly described in Chapter 1 and more technically elaborated in the Appendix. While this study is intended as a contribution to the sociology of religion and the sociology of professions, the volume was prepared primarily with the general reader in mind. Its foremost objective is to provide empirical grounds for the current discussions about the purpose of the church and its ministry.

At the time we initiated this survey, I was completing another study of a sample of parishioners in the United Church of Christ. The results of that survey were published in the volume, *The Fragmented Layman: An Empirical Study of*

Lay Attitudes, which I co-authored with Professor (now President) Thomas C. Campbell of the Chicago Theological Seminary. We included a number of questions from the study of laymen in our study of pastors and seminarians in order to compare attitudes of clergymen and laymen on a number of issues. In one sense *The Ministry in Transition* is a sequel to *The Fragmented Layman.* Our first volume was a sociological examination of the pew; in this volume I have turned my attention to the pulpit.[3]

Although this is a study of a single denomination, its findings are likely to be applicable to other denominations sharing the liberal and middle class characteristics of the United Church of Christ. In *The Fragmented Layman* we noted the unique ecumenical make-up of the constituency of this denomination, for only 43 per cent of the laymen in that survey grew up in either of the two denominations which formed the United Church of Christ. The majority were formerly Baptists, Lutherans, Methodists, and Presbyterians.

Of the 1,191 pastors who participated in this survey, 57 per cent reported having been raised either in the Congregational Christian churches or the Evangelical and Reformed Church. Most of the others, like the parishioners they serve, were formerly members of other denominations. Furthermore, 48 per cent of these pastors received their theological training in interdenominational schools or in seminaries related to other denominations.

The 1,283 seminarians in this study are even more ecumenical. Since seven of the thirteen seminaries affiliated with this denomination are interdenominational, only 26 per cent of the students responding to the questionnaire reported being members of the United Church of Christ. The large majority of these seminarians are Baptists, Lutherans, Methodists, and Presbyterians, and their views therefore reflect a broader spectrum of American Protestantism.

In this report I have used the classification scheme found in Professor Harrison's report to the Commission on Theological Education to distinguish between "denominational" and "interdenominational" seminaries. In one sense all thirteen schools are "denominational," since all are officially related to the United Church of Christ. However, for historic and other reasons, denominational seminaries are more or less dependent on resources of the denomination for support, while interdenominational schools are independent of such support. Most of the interdenominational seminaries are also related to major universities.[4]

The following table shows the distribution of responses from pastors and seminarians according to the four types of seminaries in which ministers of the United Church of Christ are trained:

Distribution of Responses by Seminary Groups.

Seminary Group and Seminary	Number of Responses Pastors	Number of Responses Seminarians
All responses	1,191	1,283
Evangelical and Reformed Seminaries (E & R)	360	187
Eden Theological Seminary	173	77
Lancaster Theological Seminary	140	66
United Theological Seminary	47	44
Congregational Christian Seminaries (C C)	257	337
Andover-Newton Theological School	120	185
Bangor Theological Seminary	68	58
Chicago Theological Seminary	69	94
Interdenominational Seminaries (IND)	276	759
Hartford Seminary Foundation	46	68
Harvard University Divinity School	30	114
Howard University School of Religion	2	19
Pacific School of Religion	49	52
Union Theological Seminary	52	230
Vanderbilt University Divinity School	6	85
Yale University Divinity School	91	191
Seminaries of Other Denominations	298	

In the following chapters the data will be presented around a number of themes related to our general focus on the ministry in this period of transition. Chapter 1 begins with a note of vocational crisis, a situation which clergymen have faced in other periods of social change and one which they now share with other professionals.

Chapter 2 examines some long-standing assumptions about the social origins of clergymen and the manner in which they are recruited. Ministers of the United Church of Christ are reared in urban places, and the ministry is not necessarily a means of upward social mobility. In spite of prevailing criticisms of the local church, the potential minister's pastor continues to be the primary role model in the recruitment process, and the local church the principal context in which the decision to become a minister is made.

The education of ministers is described in Chapter 3. The formal curricula of the seminaries as well as the major fields of study pursued by seminarians remain quite traditional. Ministers and students express a desire for change toward a curriculum more oriented to social issues, but there is also some ambivalence on their part.

Chapter 4 focuses on two aspects of the minister's work—administration and pastoral care—around which the present uncertainty of the minister's calling is analyzed. The minister's work is also described in terms of the dominant institutional structure within which he does his work—the residentially based parish church—and its relationship to his desire to work more effectively with social issues.

Chapter 5 uses data from a national survey of laymen in the United Church of Christ to explore the differences that exist between the pulpit and the pew over social issues and conceptions about the purpose of the church and its ministry. Ministers were found to be oriented toward cognitive and action forms of ministry, while the laity desire affective ministries that will serve their personal and family needs. There is also a latent clericalism, in that clergymen tend to favor programs over which they exercise primary leadership, while laymen favor those over which they have some measure of control. While clergymen and laymen are divided over controversial social issues, there is little evidence of polarization in the sense that laymen exhibit no real consensus about particular issues or modes of appropriate church action.

Chapter 6 is addressed to the problem of church unity. The data for this study were collected ten years after the union of the Evangelical and Reformed Church and the Congregational Christian Churches to form the United Church of Christ. There is evidence of the persistence of denominationalism a decade after the union, suggesting the salience of H. Richard Niebuhr's theory about the social sources of denominationalism in America. These differences also account for different styles of education and ministry in the United Church of Christ.

The final chapter summarizes the findings along two dimensions: from a sociological perspective within a theory of the professions, and from the perspective of religion through an elaboration of a theory of the ministry. Three basic styles of education and ministry are described: the institutional style, oriented toward the denomination; the individualistic style, oriented toward the parishioner; and the social style, which is oriented toward society. These types prevail as alternative modes of education and ministry for the professional leadership of the United Church of Christ.

The research reported in these pages was made possible by the cooperation and contributions of many people. We are grateful most of all to the nearly 2,500 pastors and seminarians who took the time to respond to our questionnaire. Because they are nameless, our indebtedness to them can never be adequately expressed.

The major share of the funding for this research was provided by the United Church Board for Homeland Ministries through its Division of Higher Education and the American Missionary Association. I wish to express my special thanks to the Division's General Secretary, Wesley A. Hotchkiss, whose encouragement and support through all stages of the project have made the publication of this volume possible. Additional financial support was also provided by the Central Research Fund of the College of Liberal Arts at The Pennsylvania State University.

My wife, Toshiko Fukuyama, was responsible for preparing the original data cards and tabulations, a task she performed with accuracy and speed. Ruth L. Sprague and Theodore A. McConnell read the manuscript in its early form and provided me with many helpful suggestions from their perspectives as educators and editors. One of my graduate students, William J. McKinney, Jr., also read the manuscript, and his comments from the viewpoint of a recent seminary graduate were particularly timely and helpful. I have already mentioned the very important part my colleague Paul M. Harrison played in the initial stages of this research; my indebtedness to him is very great.

For both personal and professional reasons, I am particularly grateful to Davie Napier for preparing the Foreword to this volume. I first met Dr. Napier when he was on the faculty of the Divinity School of Yale University. In the mid-1960s he became the chaplain and professor at Stanford University, and in 1971 he was called to his present position as President of the Pacific School of Religion. His wide-ranging professional experiences have touched directly many of the themes discussed in this study, making his contribution uniquely appropriate.

I have dedicated this book to Truman B. Douglass, who was until shortly before his death in 1969 the Executive Vice President of the United Church Board for Homeland Ministries. He was a pastor's pastor, a sagacious teacher, an eloquent preacher, an imaginative administrator, and a courageous prophet. Most of all, he was a warm and trusted friend.

YOSHIO FUKUYAMA

University Park, Pennsylvania
Spring, 1972

1

The Uncertain Calling

The decade of the seventies will be one in which most of the traditional institutions of American society will be both challenged and transformed in ways undreamed of during other periods of social change. The American railroad industry, which symbolized the vigor of the free enterprise system and made possible the development of our industrial strength and the growth of our cities in the past century, is on the verge of bankruptcy and nationalization. Radical protest in recent years has challenged our military, governmental, educational, health, and welfare systems in unprecedented ways. We are becoming increasingly sensitized to the paradox of the world's wealthiest nation whose health care and delivery system is archaic and inadequate; a new breed of professors and students is confronting our universities and their traditional elitist style of higher education.

Less dramatic, though none the less significant, has been the slow erosion of traditional work styles as a result of increasing technology and automation. Auto mechanics no longer repair automobiles; they are trained to replace parts. Each year large metropolitan dailies close down, for their traditional hegemony over the distribution of news has been drastically reduced by the electronic news media. The unskilled worker, both on the farm and in the factory, is being made obsolete by numerous labor-saving devices, and the neighborhood grocer with his ball of twine and scale has long since been replaced by prepackaged products and the checkout counter. Even the housewife is no longer the canner of food and the baker of bread. Her electric kitchen and freezer have transformed her role.

The religious sector has also been in ferment. The churches' protest against traditionalism has differed from the protest over war, racism, education, and unresponsive government in that it has not been marked by the overt violence that has accompanied other kinds of protest. Furthermore, the churches' protest has come largely from within the institution rather than from outside it; much of the leadership for change and the development of new forms of ministry have also come from within the churches.

One could argue in this context that the history of the Christian churches is in itself a history of protest and change, and from this perspective overt violence has sometimes occurred. In the sixteenth century, Luther's protest against the traditionalism of the medieval Church led to the Peasants' Revolt; Roger Williams' banishment from Massachusetts in the seventeenth century was a response to traditional conceptions of both the Church and its ministry.

While protest and change are not new, each period has its own focus of protest and sources of change. Our concern is primarily with the clergyman and how he is prepared for his profession in contemporary society.

In 1956, in a well-known study of theological education sponsored by the Carnegie Corporation, H. Richard Niebuhr defined the basic problem in these words:

> . . . the contemporary Church is confused about the nature of the ministry. Neither ministers nor the schools that nurture them are guided today by a clear-cut, generally accepted conception of the office of the ministry, though such an idea may be emerging.[1]

Niebuhr went on to observe that this confusion about the conception of the ministry was pointed to some 20 years previously by W. A. Brown and Mark A. May in their four-volume report, *The Education of American Ministers.*[2]

More recently, James D. Glasse, now president of Lancaster Theological Seminary, has written about "a crisis among the American clergy" and characterized it as a crisis in "identity."[3]

In its annual issue devoted to theological education, the editors of *The Christian Century* in 1971 began with the following words: "Protestant seminaries are drying on the vine and Catholic seminaries are dying on the vine."[4] The issue, they argued, is economic, for the recent years have seen significant curricular innovation and experimental programs, and some seminaries have been depicted as being new centers of student revolt and dissent.

The crisis in theological education is not apparent when one reads the display advertisements in this special issue of the *Century.* "A Bold New Venture in Theological Studies" reads one such advertisement. Another characterizes its program as "challenging, relevant academic preparation for the parish integrated with an extensive supervised program of field education—pastoral, clinical, and social."

In a feature article, Browne Barr, pastor of the First Congregational Church in Berkeley, California, argues that "drastic radical reform of education for the parish ministry is long overdue." After taking note of the important work done by distinguished seminaries in the recent past, Dr. Barr concludes that "all this work is being done in schools originally established for the training of ministers for local congregations."[5]

Barr's point is that the original role of the seminaries—that of training ministers for the parish ministry—has become peripheral, if not lost, in their preoccupation with more "relevant" ministries.

Whether one chooses to define the problem in terms of the

church's confusion about the nature of the ministry, the identity crisis of clergymen, or the failure of seminaries to train pastors for the parish, there can be no doubt about the uncertainty of the minister's calling today. Let us turn to some empirical evidence to examine the extent of this vocational crisis and its underlying causes.

The data supporting our observations will be presented in a series of tables, in most instances reporting findings separately for pastors and seminarians. Within each table, the results will also be differentiated according to the type of seminary attended by the respondent. Percentages have been rounded off to the nearest whole number, and chi-square tests, where appropriate, will give the reader an indication of the level at which the relationships reported in each table are significant.[6]

Attitudes toward the Parish Ministry

The vocational crisis in the church is to be seen first in terms of the location of one's professional activities, and second in terms of the profession itself. The uncertainty of one's calling to be a minister is greater for the seminarian than it is for the pastor; it is greater for those who receive their theological education in interdenominational schools than for those who are educated in denominational institutions.

Fifty-seven per cent of the 1,191 ministers who responded to our questionnaire thought that they would like to be working in the parish ministry "five or ten years from now." As Table 1–1 shows, interest in the parish ministry was most frequently reported by ministers who attended former Evangelical and Reformed seminaries, and least frequently reported by those who received their training in interdenominational schools.

Of all the ministers responding, 82 per cent were actually serving parish churches at the time the survey was conducted.

Table 1–1 Type of Vocation Anticipated by Pastors after Five or Ten Years (by type of seminary background).

Type of Vocation	Per Cent Responding Total	E & R	C C	Ind	Other
Number reporting	1,191	360	257	276	298
Parish ministry	57	65	57	49	55
College teaching	11	7	10	16	13
Ecumenical work	10	9	12	13	9
Campus ministry	6	3	7	9	6
Seminary teaching	6	6	3	7	7
Other professional work	6	6	6	4	7
Denominational work	5	5	5	3	4
Nonmilitary chaplaincy	4	4	4	4	4
Military chaplaincy	2	2	3	1	3
Other	10	8	12	13	10

Table 1–2 Type of Vocation Anticipated by Seminarians after Five or Ten Years (by type of seminary background).

Type of Vocation	Per Cent Responding Total	E & R	C C	Ind
Number reporting	1,283	187	337	759
Parish ministry	37	57	41	30
College teaching	25	10	15	33
Campus ministry	11	7	12	11
Seminary teaching	11	8	9	12
Ecumenical work	7	4	8	6
Other professional work	7	2	7	8
Nonmilitary chaplaincy	4	7	7	2
Denominational work	3	4	6	2
Military chaplaincy	2	4	2	1
Other	13	12	14	13

As a group, seven ministers out of ten chose to remain in the parish ministry "five or ten years from now."

Interest in the parish church as the location of one's ministry is significantly lower among students who are now training for the ministry than it is for ministers who are now engaged in professional activities. In Table 1–2 we find that only 37 per cent of the 1,283 seminarians responding thought that they would like to be working in parish churches "five or ten years from now." Again, interest in this type of vocation was highest for students attending former Evangelical and Reformed schools (57 per cent) and lowest for those enrolled in interdenominational seminaries (30 per cent). For the latter group, fully one-third thought that they would like to be in "college teaching," and another 12 per cent selected "seminary teaching" as the location of their work in the future.

If there is uncertainty about the parish ministry as the location of one's professional work, there is even more uncertainty about the ministry itself. For only three respondents in ten—both ministers and students—"the idea of entering some vocation other than the ministry" was reported to have "little or no appeal." For 66 per cent of the ministers and 69 per cent of the seminarians, such a notion was "strong" or "sometimes" appealing.

We note in Tables 1–3 and 1–4 that disenchantment with the ministry as a vocation is most salient for respondents educated in interdenominational seminaries. Seventy-three per cent of the pastors and 75 per cent of the students related to these schools find the notion of entering some other vocation than the ministry to be strongly or sometimes appealing. It is of further interest to note that currently enrolled students in the former Evangelical and Reformed seminaries are less uncertain about the ministry as a vocation than pastors who attended these schools. Forty per cent of the ministers, compared with 46 per cent of the students, found "little or no appeal" in the notion of leaving their chosen profession.

Table 1–3 Attitude of Pastors toward Leaving the Ministry (by type of seminary attended).

The idea of entering some vocation other than the ministry	Per Cent Responding				
	Total	E & R	C C	Ind	Other
Number reporting	1,191	360	257	276	298
Still has a strong appeal to me	21	15	22	26	24
Sometimes appeals to me	45	45	47	47	42
Has little or no appeal for me	33	40	30	27	34

Chi square = 20.5516; $df = 6$; p = less than .002.

Table 1–4 Attitude of Seminarians toward Leaving the Ministry (by type of seminary attended).

The idea of entering some vocation other than the ministry	Per Cent Responding			
	Total	E & R	C C	Ind
Number reporting	1,283	187	337	759
Still has a strong appeal to me	32	13	26	40
Sometimes appeals to me	37	41	40	35
Has little or no appeal for me	31	46	34	25

Chi square = 65.4704; $df = 4$; p = less than .001.

While our data suggest a serious crisis in vocational commitment, we believe it is rooted primarily in the location and style of the minister's work rather than in his personal commitment to his profession. He is anxious about his vocation because he is uncertain about the institution in which he does his work.

We asked our respondents to indicate "the *one* personal decision which is most pressing" at the present time. Both pastors and seminarians were agreed about the order in which the issues confronted them, though they did not always agree about the intensity of the issues. Let us examine their responses as given in Table 1–5, in which the items are listed in the order of their frequencies.

We see here that the "most pressing" decision facing both the ministers and students centers essentially around "the purpose of the church and its ministry." Following that, both

Table 1–5 Personal Decision Considered to be the "Most Pressing."

Type of Decision	Per Cent Responding: Pastors	Per Cent Responding: Seminarians
Number reporting	1,191	1,283
The purpose of the church and its ministry	41	29
Nature of my personal involvement in controversial social issues	16	15
Commitment to institutional Christianity	13	14
The ministry as the vocation for me	10	11
My search for personal identity	7	13
Commitment to Christianity	5	8
Other	8	9

Chi square = 52.4355; $df = 6$; p = less than .001.

groups mentioned the nature of their personal involvement in controversial social issues and their "commitment to institutional Christianity."

The primary locus of the respondents' concerns appears to be more institutional than personal; decisions having to do with one's personal identity and commitment are less pressing than those having to do with the institution in which they work.

This is expressed in their responses to the question, "What

is your general attitude and feeling toward the existing form of the local residential parish church?" We selected this particular form of the ministry because it is the predominant context in which clergymen do their work. We find in Table 1–6 that the majority of the ministers are positive in their attitude, while nearly half of the students are critical.

Table 1–6 Attitude toward "The Existing Form of the Parish Church."

Attitude toward parish church	Per Cent Responding Pastors	Seminarians
Number reporting	1,191	1,283
Strongly supportive	25	15
Moderately or ambiguously supportive	32	29
Neutral	3	4
Moderately or ambiguously critical	25	31
Strongly critical	13	18
Other	3	3

Chi square = 50.1894; *df* = 5; *p* = less than .001.

While 57 per cent of the pastors are moderately or strongly supportive of the existing form of the residential parish church, only 44 per cent of the students now training for the ministry share this view. Yet, when asked to indicate "what type of ministry [the respondent is] best equipped to serve," two-thirds of the ministers and 45 per cent of the seminarians identified the role of the "parish pastor."

In a later chapter we will describe more fully the bases of this vocational anxiety about the work of the minister. Our present concern is simply to underscore the fact that the ministry today is facing a crisis in vocation, and that this crisis is focused on the purpose of the church and the minister's proper place in it.

In 1968, *McCall's Magazine* reported on a survey conducted by Ardis Whitman in which more than 3,000 ministers responded to questions concerning their work. Our data confirm many of the observations made by Mrs. Whitman. For example:

> . . . Ministers of all ages saw the church with a mixture of exasperation and love. But older men, for the most part, had made their peace philosophically with its imperfections and were more likely to talk about a sense of calling and a feeling that the church was in some special way the vehicle of God's word.
>
> Not so the young. . . .[7]

While her research population of Protestant ministers is considerably broader than ours, her conclusions are remarkably similar:

> . . . Ministers in general seem to spend a lot of time thinking of leaving. More than two thirds of the total sample said they had thought of it. . . . nearly half of all ministers in their twenties and thirties—and a not substantially smaller group in their forties—had thought *seriously* of leaving the ministry as against less than twenty-five percent of the oldest group.[8]

According to Mrs. Whitman, the basic reason for thinking of leaving the ministry can be summed up in one word: relevance.

> Relevance to what? To the world, to life, to "where the action is," to what it is they think a Christian should be doing.[9]

In part, the clergyman's feeling of the church's irrelevance derives from a basic conflict that exists between his and his parishioners' conceptions of the church's purposes. In our survey, we asked each respondent to indicate the importance he attached to each of ten typical programs found in a residential parish church. This same question was included in a study of the laity of the United Church of Christ which was reported in an earlier publication.[10] By comparing the rankings assigned to each program by our different groups of respondents, we begin to see something of the conflict that prevails between clergymen and their parishioners.

In Table 1–7 we have excluded the intermediate rankings in order to highlight the dissonance between clergy and lay

Table 1–7 Importance of Typical Church Programs (rankings assigned by pastors, seminarians, and laymen).

Rank	Pastors	Seminarians	Laymen
1	Study groups	Study groups	Church board
2	Social action group	Social action group	Church committees
3	Retreats	Adult Sunday School	Women's groups
8	Women's groups	Church committees	Social action groups
9	Prayer meetings	Men's groups	Prayer meetings
10	Men's groups	Women's groups	Retreats

attitudes. It would appear that ministers and students are primarily oriented toward cognitive and action programs, while the laity consider organizational activities to be most important. We might hypothesize that the present discontent with the existing form of the parish church could be reduced for the clergy if the laity would become more cognitively and action oriented. Or, the minister might make the accommodation and become more organizationally oriented.

Table 1–7 also suggests a latent "clericalism" in the sense that both pastors and seminarians have ranked men's groups and women's groups at the bottom of their lists. The programs most favored by the professionals are those in which the minister assumes primary leadership as the teacher and moral leader of the community. Laymen, by contrast, place their highest priorities where their leadership is primary: in the governance of the congregation and in the women's groups.

Still another way to understand the nature of the vocational crisis in the parish is to look at the way in which traditional clergy roles are perceived and evaluated by our three respondent groups. Twelve typical clergy roles were listed in the questionnaire, and each respondent was asked first to indicate how much time he thought ministers generally spent in performing each role, and second whether he thought the minister spent "too much," "too little," or "about right" amount of time in each activity. Table 1–8 is a comparative summary of these data, showing only the items most frequently mentioned by each group. We have included the percentage of each group responding to indicate the degree to which these attitudes were expressed by the various groups in the survey.

Ministers see themselves spending "a lot of time" in "study and sermon preparation" and underscore the priority given to this role by also reporting that "too little time" is devoted to it. They also see themselves spending "a lot of time" in "office and administrative work," but they are also most critical of the amount of time they spend in performing this task.

Unlike the working pastor who sees himself primarily in his role as a preacher and comforter of the sick and bereaved, the seminarian sees him most often as an administrator and organizer. Students are not only very critical of ministers for spending "too much time" in administrative and organizational work, but are critical because "too little time" is spent in the roles of prophet, teacher, and preacher.

Laymen see their ministers primarily as ministers see themselves and, it would appear, are quite satisfied with the manner in which their ministers work. The few laymen who

Table 1–8 How Ministers Spend their Time (summary by respondent groups).

Rank	Pastors	Seminarians	Laymen
	"A Lot of time"		
1	Study and sermon preparation (48)	Office and administrative work (61)	Leading worship (60)
2	Office and administrative work (45)	Organizing church programs (50)	Study and sermon preparation (49)
3	Visiting sick and bereaved (38)	Counseling people with problems (32)	Visiting sick and bereaved (46)
	"Too much time"		
1	Office and administrative work (55)	Office and administrative work (84)	Office and administrative work (10)
2	Organizing church programs (23)	Raising money for the church (61)	Working for social justice (5)
3	Raising money for the church (10)	Organizing church programs (56)	Raising money for the church (5)
	"Too little time"		
1	Working for social justice (56)	Working for social justice (78)	Calling on members (15)
2	Study and sermon preparation (51)	Teaching (74)	Working with children and youth (10)
3	Calling on nonmembers (48)	Study and sermon preparation (68)	Calling on nonmembers (10)

Per cent responding in parentheses.

express criticism do so only in terms of more calling on and attention to parishioners and prospective church members.

To summarize, much of the disenchantment felt by ministers and theological students with the residential parish church is caused by a conflict between what clergymen think they ought to be doing and what they are actually spending their time doing. Most ministers see themselves primarily as preachers and pastors; they find themselves functioning for the most part as administrators and organizers. They also like to see themselves as champions of social justice, a role which ranks among the lowest for the laity, but they admit to spending very little time in this way.

Similar observations were made in 1956 by Samuel W. Blizzard in his study of 1,111 clergymen, sponsored by the Russell Sage Foundation. Blizzard's respondents ranked clergy roles in the following normative order: preacher, pastor, priest (leader of worship), teacher, organizer, and administrator. When their roles were ranked according to the amount of time spent on each, quite a different ordering resulted: administrator, pastor, preacher, organizer, and teacher.[11]

Role conflict for the clergyman, it would appear, is a persistent one.

The Problem of Role Definition

An assumption is often made that the principal reason for the contemporary minister's role conflict resides in the fact "that the activities of the clergy in the United States are increasing in number and variety."[12] This is the thesis suggested by James M. Gustafson's essay, "The Clergy in the United States," which appeared in an issue of *Daedalus* devoted to "The Professions." Professor Gustafson describes the traditional responsibilities of the clergy in the following way:

> For what is the clergyman responsible? The traditional answers are rather clear. He is responsible for the religious life of the

> members of his congregation or parish, for the preservation and propagation of his religious tradition, for the administration of the means of grace, for the application of moral and religious law, for the maintenance and growth of religious organizations, for the moral well-being of the society and for the spiritual needs of individual persons. These responsibilities are exercised in traditional roles of the clergyman. He is the preacher, the scholar and teacher, the priest at the altar, the moral and spiritual counselor. . . .[13]

He goes on to add that the American clergyman today is responsible for many other things:

> . . . the behavior of his youth group on a bowling party, the conduct of a financial campaign for a building fund, the public relations of the parish church, the effectiveness of the local council of churches or ministerial association, mitigating tensions between conflicting groups in the community, saying the blessing at the service club luncheon, the sex education of adolescents, premarital counseling, and many more.[14]

Contrast this many-faceted function of the modern minister with Wilhelm Pauck's description of the clergyman's task in the time of the Continental Reformation:

> The primary ministerial function was *preaching*. And what a load of it the ministers of the era of the Reformation had to carry! In his *German Mass* Luther described the practice prevailing at Wittenberg as follows: On Sunday, there were three services. At the early morning service, at five or six o'clock, there was a sermon on the Epistle of the day. At the main service, at eight or nine o'clock, the minister preached on the Gospel of the day. The sermon at the Vesper service in the afternoon was based on the Old Testament. It was the practice to expound the whole book consecutively, Sunday after Sunday. Monday and Tuesday were the days of the Catechism. . . . The early morning service on Wednesday was centered on the Gospel of Matthew. On Thursday and Friday, the Epistles were expounded. On Saturday, a late afternoon Vesper service was held, and the Gospel of John traditionally furnished the text of the sermon. In other places the practice was similar.[15]

During the century following the Reformation, the pulpit remained central in defining the minister's role. In addition to his responsibilities for preaching, conducting public worship, and administering the sacraments, the Puritan minister took on additional pastoral duties which included catechizing, visiting, disciplining, and counseling the members of his flock. The proliferation of the minister's responsibilities in the Puritan Age is characterized by Winthrop S. Hudson in the following account:

> It was a busy life these [Puritan] parsons led. . . . On Sundays, there were two services with preaching in the morning and catechizing in the afternoon. . . . On weekdays, the afternoons were utilized "to visit in person, now one quarter of the parish, now another," to counsel, admonish, and exhort. . . . The mornings were for reading and study and the numerous other activities which were the pastor's lot. Mealtimes were the occasion for extending the hospitality of the table to his parishioners, taking them in turn. . . . Not infrequently he was called upon to serve as schoolmaster to the parish children, and occasionally . . . for the instruction of adults as well. . . . Nor was it unusual for a clergyman to be licensed to practice medicine, and whether licensed or not he was expected to keep a book of "physic" at hand and his wife a garden of medicinal herbs. . . . In similar fashion, he needed at least an elementary knowledge of law, for as the educated person of the community he was called upon to give legal advice, draft legal documents, and frequently adjudicate legal disputes. . . . he needed a moderate knowledge of farming . . . and able to handle a plow and a spade with reasonable skill.[16]

Religion on the American frontier was normatively defined by John Wesley's classic admonition to his preachers: "You have nothing to do but save souls." However, the voluntarism of religious life in America, together with the social impact of the nineteenth century, which brought immigration, industrialization, and urbanization, continued to challenge and redefine the responsibilities of the clergyman. While the evangelical ideal of the conversion of sinners was kept in sight, numerous functionaries of the church developed: evangelists and revivalists, parish ministers and teachers, missionaries and secretaries of societies, specialized ministers for the city immigrant and the rural poor.

What this brief historical survey suggests is that while the contemporary minister may find his responsibilities to be numerous and varied, his situation is not without precedent. The essential problem is to determine the priorities to be assigned to the various demands made on the minister's time and to make sure that he is adequately prepared to carry out his responsibilities with both skill and satisfaction.

The Survey Design

This case study of the ministry in transition is based on a survey conducted in 1967. The technical details of the survey design are found in the methodological Appendix at the conclusion of this volume. In order to understand the empirical foundation on which the following chapters rest, it is necessary to summarize briefly the characteristics of those whose responses will be reported.

There are three distinct survey populations included in this study. The first two—pastors and seminarians—constitute the core data and are derived from the study of theological education described in the Preface. A total of 1,191 pastors and 1,283 seminarians returned usable questionnaires.

In presenting these data, distinctions will be made between responses from pastors and those from theological students. In addition, we have also made distinctions between several types of seminaries in which ministers of the United Church of Christ receive their training. Three of the thirteen seminaries were formerly identified with the Evangelical and Reformed Church (Eden, Lancaster, and United) and three with the Congregational Christian Churches (Andover-Newton, Bangor, and Chicago). The remaining seven are identified in the study as "interdenominational" seminaries.

Since many pastors of this denomination received their theological training in seminaries related to other denominations, a fourth category labeled "other" is used in the analysis. This category is not relevant for the seminarian responses.

A third survey population comes from a study of the laymen in the United Church of Christ, which was conducted shortly before this study of theological education. Responses from 8,549 laymen were received in that survey, and the findings were reported in the volume *The Fragmented Layman* in 1970. The data from this study is particularly important for our discussion of "The Gap Between Pulpit and Pew," Chapter 5.

We will now turn to three basic themes in our study of theological education: who are recruited for the ministry, how are they trained for their profession, and how do clergymen perceive their work?

2

Sources of Clergy Recruitment

Who are the men and women who choose the ministry as a vocation? It is generally acknowledged by historians of theological education that the minister achieved his highest prominence in Puritan New England, where he was not only the best educated member of the community, but also enjoyed high prestige and power. Professors Brown and May in 1934 studied the educational backgrounds of Congregational ministers in New England from the Colonial period to this century and concluded that "the educational level of the Protestant ministry in the United States in 1926 was below that of 100 years ago and well below that of 200 years ago."[1]

In 1954, Richard A. La Piere, a sociologist, made the following observation:

> . . . A hundred years ago the Protestant ministry was a profession of high prestige and equally high morale; it then drew to it men of intellectual vigor and strong ambition. Today the ministry is a profession as low in prestige as in income, and the general level of morale among ministers is lower still; today, therefore, the university training centers for the ministry get the culls of the academic crop.[2]

Professor La Piere did not provide empirical documentation for his conclusions, though his viewpoint is a persistent and popular one.

Undoubtedly, the social status ascribed to a profession will have some consequence for determining the type of person who is recruited. One indicator of our interest in the minister's social status is the intensive discussion about degree nomenclature within the American Association of Theological Schools. Another is the debate over the "professional" versus "vocational" nature of the ministry. Other issues, such as the minister's educational requirements, his salary, and his opportunities for advancement and growth, are aspects of his status.

Comparative studies of occupational status are difficult to assess because most studies use different categories of professions. In one study reported by Robert W. Hodge and his colleagues, ministers shared the ranking of 17 with the psychologists, below that of lawyers (11) and architects (14), but ahead of civil engineers (21) and sociologists (26). At the top of this list were U.S. Supreme Court Justices (1), physicians (2), and scientists (3).

These rankings were based on data collected in 1963. Comparable data gathered in 1947 had ranked ministers 13th in status, which reflects a decline in the clergyman's status during the intervening fifteen-year period.[3]

Social status is, of course, a function of cultural values. In another study, occupational status was compared for several nations. In the United States, ministers ranked below physicians, college professors, and scientists, but above architects and lawyers. In Germany, university professors ranked first, followed by physicians and high civil servants, with the minister (*Pfarrer*) coming next in order. In Japan, the priests of Buddhist temples ranked below elementary school teachers and newspaper reporters.[4]

For Americans, higher education is a major cultural value. The rankings assigned to various occupational groups are in part related to the educational requirement for each group. In 1960, the U.S. Census of Population reported that clergymen as a group completed a median of 17.1 years of school, ranking fifth behind physicians (17.5), lawyers (17.4), college professors (17.4) and secondary school teachers (17.2).[5]

We would argue on the basis of these observations that while the contemporary Protestant minister does not enjoy the preeminent status of his Puritan forebears, his profession is still esteemed in American society. A better indicator of his present status is to examine the characteristics of our research population so that empirically valid statements can be made to assess the quality of those who choose the ministry as a profession.

Before turning to our data, we will take account of several observations made by Protestant leaders in recent years suggesting the sources of recruitment for the ministry. We intend to treat these observations as hypotheses to be tested empirically with our data.

Professor James M. Gustafson of Yale Divinity School has observed that "Judgments about the quality of men who enter the ministry are difficult to make."[6] In his very instructive monograph, "The Clergy in the United States," which appeared in 1963, he went on to make the following comments:

> Among Protestants there are two notable trends in recent years among students who enroll as seminarians. One is the increase in the number of students who are vocationally uncertain at the time of admission. Indeed, many of them are uncertain about their religious convictions and commitment. . . . A second trend is for men who have established themselves in other occupations to engage in theological study and to become ministers.[7]

Another persistent theme about ministerial recruitment is rooted in Protestantism's seeming ineffectiveness in its ministry to the city. Truman B. Douglass, a prominent home missions executive, wrote these words for *Harper's Magazine:*

> In more recent years [Protestantism's] alienation from the life of the city has been accentuated by the rural origins and outlook of its ministry. Protestant ministers are disproportionately drawn from the smaller communities, disproportionately trained in the

> small colleges of the South and Midwest. . . . Because of their rural and small-town origins, many ministers bring to their work in a city church a distaste for city ways—a distaste which is more disabling because it is largely unconscious.[8]

Dr. Douglass' assertion about the rural and small-town origins of Protestant clergymen was supported as recently as 1965 by the findings of a study of preseminary education sponsored by the Lilly Foundation. For the modal seminarian, "the community in which he grew up is described as 'farm or open country.' "[9]

This study was based on questionnaires returned by more than 17,500 seminarians who were enrolled in Protestant seminaries in North America during the academic year 1962–1963. The directors of the study, Keith R. Bridston and Dwight W. Culver, gave the following modal "Portrait of the Pre-Seminarian":

> The Protestant seminarian is 25½ years old. He is male and white. He is married. The ministry is regarded by him as having a social standing higher than the occupation of his father, a skilled worker. His paternal grandfather was a farmer. He is an older child in a family of three children. The education of his parents is less than his own. . . .
>
> As to his religious background. . . . He was encouraged to attend Sunday school and church services. In his family, grace was said before meals. There was at least one religious periodical regularly in the home. . . . On the whole, however, he would not regard his parents "as deeply religious persons. . . ."[10]

To sum up, these writers characterize the minister as one whose status has declined over the years, and the ministry as a profession which attracts men primarily from rural areas and small towns. The ministry is further seen as a means of upward occupational mobility for persons who were brought up in conventionally "religious" surroundings. Gustafson has noted signs of vocational uncertainty among seminarians as well as an increase in the number of older students who choose to enter the ministry after having pursued other vocations.

While the questionnaire used in our survey of pastors and seminarians did not include all the variables mentioned by these writers, it included many of them. Let us turn to this data and explore the backgrounds out of which clergymen of the United Church of Christ are recruited.

Socio-Economic Background

To begin, the majority of the ministers and students grew up in large towns and cities; 40 per cent of the pastors and 36 per cent of the students were raised in rural places or in towns of less than 10,000 population. Approximately one-third of the respondents in both groups grew up in large cities (of 100,000 and more population) or their suburbs. If Protestant ministers were at one time disproportionately recruited from rural places and small towns, it is obviously no longer true, at least for the United Church of Christ. Like the population as a whole, clergymen of this denomination are predominantly urban in their upbringing.

However, within the United Church of Christ, this variable functions differently, depending on the type of seminary the respondent attended. As Tables 2–1 and 2–2 show, the proportion of those with rural or small town backgrounds is highest for those attending former Evangelical and Reformed seminaries and lowest for those educated in the interdenominational schools.

By collapsing the first two categories (rural farm and small town) in both tables, we find that half of the pastors and students attending former Evangelical and Reformed seminaries were raised in rural places and small towns, in contrast with 35 per cent of the Congregational Christian seminary alumni and students and approximately 30 per cent of those related to interdenominational schools. We also note a decrease in

Table 2–1 Type of Community in which Pastors Grew Up (by type of seminary attended).

Type of Community	Total	E & R	C C	Ind	Other
	Per Cent Responding				
Number responding (N = 100%)	1,191	360	257	276	298
Rural farm, village	20	28	10	14	24
Small town (under 10,000)	20	22	25	16	19
Medium town (10,000–49,999)	19	14	26	21	17
Small city (50,000–99,999)	8	5	7	12	8
Medium city (100,000–499,999)	11	7	10	14	13
Large city (500,000 & over)	14	18	11	12	12
Suburb of large city	9	7	11	11	7

Chi square = 84.1120; $df = 18$; p = less than .001.

Table 2–2 Type of Community in which Seminarians Grew Up (by type of seminary attended).

Type of Community	Total	E & R	C C	Ind
	Per Cent Responding			
Number responding (N = 100%)	1,283	187	337	759
Rural farm, village	15	26	13	13
Small town (under 10,000)	20	24	21	19
Medium town (10,000–49,999)	20	16	25	19
Small city (50,000–99,999)	10	5	13	10
Medium city (100,000–499,999)	13	8	10	15
Large city (500,000 & over)	10	13	8	10
Suburb of large city	12	9	10	14

Chi square = 47.9051; $df = 12$; p = less than .001.

the proportion of seminarians who grew up in rural places and a corresponding increase in the urban category when compared with ministers as a group.

Finally, we note that former Evangelical and Reformed seminaries have recruited a higher proportion of their students from large cities than have other types of seminaries. Insofar as these seminaries were identified with a major ethnic group, and since the large city has been the traditional habitat of ethnic communities, this finding confirms observations often made by urban sociologists.

The occupation of the clergyman's father is another indicator of the socio-economic background of those who become ministers. For both pastors and seminarians, half of the respondents reported that their fathers were employed in white collar occupations. Fathers employed in blue collar occupations were reported by 29 per cent of the ministers and 22 per cent of the students, while fathers engaged in farming constituted 9 per cent of the pastors and 6 per cent of the students responding.

The calling to be a minister has traditionally been considered a means of upward social mobility for the sons of the socially and economically deprived. In the Middle Ages, a significant number of clergy were recruited from the peasantry. According to Wilhelm Pauck, while a large number of Reformation preachers were recruited from the ranks of the small burghers, others were formerly "clerks, printers, typesetters, and weavers."[11] We have already noted in Bridston and Culver's study of the preseminarian that the modal seminarian regarded the ministry "as having a social standing higher than the occupation of his father."[12]

We asked the pastors and students in our survey to compare the "prestige or social status of your father's usual occupation with that of the Protestant minister today." In asking this question, we wanted to assess the salience of the ministry as a means of upward social mobility among seminarians today. The results reported in Tables 2–3 and 2–4 suggest that the ministry is becoming less significant as a means of upward mobility, though it appears to be more significant for those attending denominational seminaries than for those enrolled in interdenominational schools.

In comparing the responses from pastors and seminarians, we note first that 56 per cent of the pastors reported that the

Table 2–3 Pastors' Evaluation of Father's Occupational Status with that of the Minister (by type of seminary attended).

Compared with the Ministry my father's occupation	Per Cent Responding				
	Total	E & R	C C	Ind	Other
Number responding	1,171	350	256	271	294
. . . has higher status	12	6	12	18	13
. . . has about the same status	32	30	33	36	31
. . . has lower status	56	64	55	45	57

Chi square = 34.0732; *df* = 6; *p* = less than .001.

Table 2–4 Seminarians' Evaluation of Father's Occupational Status with that of the Minister (by type of seminary attended).

Compared with the Ministry my father's occupation	Per Cent Responding			
	Total	E & R	C C	Ind
Number responding	1,247	183	331	733
. . . has higher status	19	11	16	23
. . . has about the same status	39	35	41	40
. . . has lower status	41	54	43	37

Chi square = 22.3101; *df* = 4; *p* = less than .001.

occupation of their fathers was of a lower social status than their own, while 41 per cent of the seminarians expressed this view. Furthermore, nearly one seminarian in five (19 per cent) reported that their fathers' occupations were more prestigious than that of the clergyman, in contrast to only 6 per cent of the ordained ministers who expressed this view. Given the value assumptions implicit in the American social status system, entering the ministry was, for the majority of the pastors, a means of upward social mobility; for the majority of the present generation of theological students, entering the ministry would not serve to improve their status.

However, when responses to this question are examined in relation to the different types of seminaries attended by our respondents, we find that the ministry as a means of upward social mobility is more salient for those attending denominational seminaries than for those who have attended the ecumenical schools. Only 6 per cent of the pastors who attended Evangelical and Reformed seminaries considered the occupation of their fathers to be higher than their own, while pastors who attended interdenominational seminaries were three times more likely (18 per cent) to make this assessment. Those who attended former Congregational Christian seminaries occupied an intermediate position, along with those who attended seminaries related to other denominations.

Responses from students showed the same differences. For all groups, the father's occupation was proportionately higher in social status than that reported by pastors. A large proportion of students currently enrolled in former Evangelical and Reformed schools reported that their fathers' occupation was lower than that of the minister, while students in ecumenical seminaries were least likely to express this view. As in the case with ministers, students enrolled in Congregational Christian seminaries occupied in intermediate position between these two extremes.

We would summarize the socio-economic background of

clergymen recruited by the United Church of Christ as follows: the majority of our respondents were raised in urban places and came out of homes in which the father was a white collar worker. Traditional notions about the recruitment of Protestant ministers "from farms and small towns" and of the ministry as a means of upward social mobility are not supported by our data. A discernible shift toward a greater degree of urbanization and higher socio-economic status is suggested by the two generations represented in our survey.

Religious Background

In recent years we have witnessed a plethora of books and articles critical of the local parish church, written by people both within and without the parish ministry. The preoccupation in these writings with "relevance" and "new forms of ministry" at all levels of church organization, including the seminaries, suggests that the traditional form of church organization is at best problematical. We have already noted in Chapter 1 that a significant proportion of both pastors and seminarians are critical of "the existing form of the parish church," and that there is a conflict between the clergyman's conception of the purpose of the church and its ministry and that of the laity.

In the light of such observations, we wanted to learn how the local church actually related to those who were called to become ministers. One might assume that without a supportive local church background, recruitment for the ministry would be unlikely. We asked each respondent to characterize his "own religious background through high school" along a continuum ranging from "very secular or unchurched" to "very active and a leader."

Tables 2–5 and 2–6 show that active church relationships were not only reported by the majority of the ministers and students, but that seminarians as a group reported a higher

Table 2–5 Religious Background of Pastors through High School (by type of seminary attended).

Religious Background	Per Cent Responding Total	E & R	C C	Ind	Other
Number responding	1,191	360	257	276	298
Very secular or unchurched	6	2	7	8	7
Nominally church related	10	6	14	9	10
Average church relationship	18	20	19	18	16
Active church relationship	34	44	30	27	34
Very active and a leader	32	29	30	38	33

Chi square $= 45.9817$; $df = 12$; $p =$ less than .001.

Table 2–6 Religious Background of Seminarians through High School (by type of seminary attended).

Religious Background	Per Cent Responding Total	E & R	C C	Ind
Number responding	1,283	187	337	759
Very secular or unchurched	4	1	4	4
Nominally church related	8	11	10	7
Average church relationship	16	24	17	14
Active church relationship	29	31	31	28
Very active and a leader	43	34	38	47

Chi square $= 26.2297$; $df = 8$; $p =$ less than .001.

degree of local church involvement during their youth than the pastors. While two-thirds of the ministers reported "active" or "very active" church backgrounds, 72 per cent of the students responded in these categories.

The response "very active and a leader" was reported most

frequently by pastors and seminarians attending interdenominational schools and least often by those attending former Evangelical and Reformed seminaries. This particular finding is a reversal of another kind of assumption we often make about the role of religion in American society. Arthur J. Vidich and Joseph Bensman, in their now classic study of *Small Town and Mass Society,* characterized Springdalers' image of themselves as "a community of religious minded people" and city churches as "centers of atheism and secularism."[13] Rural and small-town folk like themselves are "more religious" than urban dwellers.

If this generalization were true, we would have expected students attending former Evangelical and Reformed seminaries to have had significantly more active local church backgrounds than those attending ecumenical schools, since a larger proportion of the former grew up in rural places and small towns than the latter. In Tables 2–1 and 2–2 we noted that 50 per cent of the pastors and students attending Evangelical and Reformed seminaries grew up in rural places and small towns, in contrast with 30 per cent of the pastors and 31 per cent of the students attending interdenominational schools. Our data show that those raised in small towns and rural places were *less* active in local churches than those who grew up in urban places.

We need to remember, too, that while interdenominational respondents had more active church backgrounds, they were also more critical than others of the "existing form of the parish church" and most uncertain about the parish ministry as a vocation.

We would add parenthetically that while our data do not show consistent relationships, when the respondent's religious background is held constant and used as a predictor of the type of seminary he attends, there is some evidence to suggest that those who have had secular or nominal church backgrounds are more likely to have attended Congregational

Christian seminaries and less likely to have attended Evangelical and Reformed schools.

The supportive role played by the respondents' local church experiences is seen further in the responses given to a question concerning persons who were helpful in making the decision to enter the ministry. Who are the "significant others," or role models, who influence one's choice of a professional career? Tables 2–7 and 2–8 rank the responses in the order of the frequency with which the particular individual was thought to be "very helpful" in making the decision to become a minister.

For both ministers and students, "my pastor at home" ranks first in order of frequency, though the pastor's role is somewhat ambiguous for the various seminary groups among student respondents. Military chaplains rank lowest among the options presented for both groups, but this is in part because only 32 per cent of the pastors and 14 per cent of the students have served in the armed forces. Denominational leaders also rank low among individuals who have been "very helpful" to our respondents in making their vocational choice.

When rankings are examined according to the type of seminary attended by those surveyed, some significant differences appear. For both pastors and seminarians attending former Evangelical and Reformed seminaries, the order is the same: pastor, spouse, and parents. For ministers who attended Congregational Christian seminaries or seminaries of other denominations, the order is: pastor, spouse, and friend. Present day students of the former Congregational Christian seminaries rank "friend" at the top of their list.

For pastors and students attending interdenominational theological schools, the role played by the campus pastor or college teacher is more important than that of parents, spouse, and/or friends. That campus pastors and college teachers are located in the academic community also suggests that inter-

Table 2–7 Persons Reported to be "Very Helpful" to Pastors in Making Vocational Decision (by type of seminary attended).

	Per Cent Responding				
Person who was "very helpful"	Total	E & R	C C	Ind	Other
Number reporting	1,191	360	257	276	298
My pastor at home	51	58	54	40	51
My spouse	38	40	35	30	45
A friend	32	30	33	27	37
A college teacher	26	24	20	22	16
My parent (s)	26	32	21	21	25
A youth leader	18	16	20	22	16
My campus pastor	17	9	16	28	16
A denominational leader	14	14	13	11	16
My military chaplain	5	4	6	2	8

Table 2–8 Persons Reported to be "Very Helpful" to Seminarians in Making Vocational Decision (by type of seminary attended).

	Per Cent Responding			
Person who was "very helpful"	Total	E & R	C C	Ind
Number reporting	1,283	187	337	759
My pastor at home	35	46	36	32
A friend	34	26	39	33
A college teacher	32	23	28	35
My spouse	26	30	35	21
My campus pastor	26	10	25	30
My parent (s)	19	27	16	18
A youth leader	15	20	14	14
A denominational leader	11	13	11	11
My military chaplain	3	1	6	1

denominational rather than denominational seminaries would be chosen by these men to the extent that such schools are most likely to be related to major universities. We note further that those attending interdenominational schools were most likely to mention "college teaching" as an alternative to the ministry as a profession.

In general we would conclude that the nurture given by the local church continues to be critical in helping individuals in their decision to enter the ministry. One's pastor continues to provide a role model for the future minister, though others, like the campus minister and college teacher, are becoming more significant for contemporary seminarians. The relative importance of the spouse's role for a significant number further suggests that the decision to enter the ministry often occurs relatively late in one's college career.

The final characteristic of the religious background of our respondents is denominational origin. The United Church of Christ is a uniquely ecumenical denomination which extends beyond the two denominations that formed the union in 1957. Our previous study of the parishioners of this denomination reported in *The Fragmented Layman* that only a minority—43 per cent—of the laymen were originally members of the Evangelical and Reformed or Congregational Christian churches. According to that survey the majority of the laity in the United Church of Christ came from other denominations, particularly the Baptist, Lutheran, Methodist, and Presbyterian churches.[14]

Of the 1,191 clergymen included in this survey, 57 per cent of the pastors reported that they *first* joined either a Congregational Christian or Evangelical and Reformed church. The remainder originally joined churches of other denominations and, like the parishioners they serve, mentioned the Baptist, Lutheran, Methodist and Presbyterian denominations most frequently.

The seminary students included in this survey represent an ever greater diversity of denominational backgrounds.

Only 26 per cent of the students are members of the United Church of Christ. This is largely because seven of the thirteen seminaries related to the denomination are interdenominational in character. Indeed, the diversity of backgrounds represented by the ministry of this denomination is a function of the interdenominational context of its theological education.

While we shall explore denominational differences in greater detail in Chapter 6, we note here that 77 per cent of all pastors attending former Evangelical and Reformed seminaries were originally members of that denomination, in contrast with 51 per cent of the pastors attending former Congregational Christian seminaries who reported Congregational Christian origins.

This indicator of denominationalism is somewhat weaker for the student population in our survey. Among those currently enrolled in former Evangelical and Reformed seminaries, 55 per cent identified themselves with that denomination. Of the Congregational Christian seminarian responses, only 31 per cent reported that they were originally Congregationalists.

Pre-Seminary Educational Background

Among the pastors and seminarians we are describing, 92 per cent have earned a bachelor's degree in the arts or sciences. One respondent in eight has also earned a master's degree.

More than half of all respondents attended denominationally related colleges as undergraduates. Approximately one-fourth in both groups attended public institutions, and another fourth attended private, nonsectarian colleges and universities. Only a small minority—4 per cent of the pastors and 3 per cent of the seminarians—reported having attended municipal, city, or community colleges for their undergraduate studies.

When responses given by pastors and students are compared, we find no significant differences in the proportions included in each category. The totals in Tables 2–9 and 2–10 both exceed 100 per cent because a number of respondents attended more than one type of college or university in pursuing their baccalaureate degrees.

Table 2–9 Type of Undergraduate School Attended by Pastors (by type of seminary attended).

		Per Cent Responding			
Type of College or University	Total	E & R	C C	Ind	Other
Number reporting	1,191	360	257	276	298
Municipal, city, or community	4	4	4	3	4
State	23	16	32	26	23
Private, nonsectarian	23	7	38	39	14
Denominationally related	55	76	34	37	63

Totals exceed 100 per cent because of multiple responses.

Table 2–10 Type of Undergraduate School Attended by Seminarians (by type of seminary attended).

	Per Cent Responding			
Type of College or University	Total	E & R	C C	Ind
Number reporting	1,283	187	337	759
Municipal, city, or community	3	3	5	2
State	24	27	26	22
Private, nonsectarian	26	8	29	29
Denominationally related	52	67	45	51

Totals exceed 100 per cent because of multiple responses.

However, when we examine the responses by the type of seminary attended, some important differences are evident. Three-fourths of the pastors and two-thirds of the semirians attending former Evangelical and Reformed institutions also attended denominationally related colleges as undergraduates. Those attending former Congregational Christian seminaries were least likely to have attended denominational colleges as undergraduates; only 34 per cent of the pastors and 45 per cent of the currently enrolled students did so.

While the proportion of those who attended denominational colleges decreased for the group of former Evangelical and Reformed seminaries, both the former Congregational Christian and interdenominational schools reported significant increases. If the differences shown by these two tables are indicators of generational change, the data suggest a shift in sources of ministerial recruitment on the part of some of the theological schools related to the United Church of Christ.

With the exception of the former Congregational Christian seminaries, denominational seminaries do not recruit a significant number of their students from private, nonsectarian colleges. None of the seminaries recruits a significant number of students who have attended city, municipal, or community colleges.

As undergraduates, the humanities and the social sciences dominated as major fields of study for both pastors and seminarians (Table 2–11). Pastors reported that they majored most often in Language-Literature-History, followed by the Social Sciences and Philosophy or Ethics. Religion was the fourth most frequently reported undergraduate major.

Like the pastors, students also reported Language-Literature-History to be their most frequent undergraduate major, followed by the Social Sciences, Philosophy and Ethics, and Religion. However, in contrast with ministers, the proportions majoring in Philosophy and Ethics and Religion increased, while majors in the Social Sciences decreased.

Table 2–11 Undergraduate Majors of Pastors and Seminarians

Major Field of Study	Per Cent Responding Pastors	 Seminarians
Number reporting	1,191	1,283
Language-Literature-History	35	36
Social Sciences	26	20
Philosophy-Ethics	16	18
Religion	13	18
Business Administration	4	2
Education	4	3
Biological Sciences	3	2
Physical Sciences	3	5
Art-Music-Drama	3	4
Engineering	2	1
Other	4	3

Totals exceed 100 per cent because of multiple choices.

It is clear that most of our respondents majored in the Humanities as undergraduates. Of particular interest is that, in a time of increasing social activism and concern on the part of the young, interest in the Social Sciences has decreased for seminary students, while interest in the Humanities, particularly Religion, has increased. This may suggest that the present day seminarian's social action orientation is motivated more by deeply felt theological and ethical concern than by an existential or empirical response to objective social conditions. We will pursue this theme further in Chapter 3, where we examine the manner in which ministers are educated and the way in which their seminary education is evaluated.

We turn finally to the academic quality of students recruited for the ministry. We began this chapter with one sociologist's assertion that "the university training centers for the ministry get the culls of the academic crop." It is undoubtedly true that the academic expectations of theological schools vary widely. It is also true that one's call to be a minister and the responsibility of the church to prepare him professionally cannot be confined to the candidate's undergraduate academic achievement. Furthermore, certain structural differences, such as the availability of scholarships and subsidized housing for theological students, not as widely available to law students or medical students, make it meaningless to compare the academic quality of seminarians with other professional students.

We can, however, investigate this problem empirically with our survey population. We asked each respondent to tell us what academic honors he received as an undergraduate. While the categories used in our questionnaire do not exhaust the criteria available, we believe they are indicators that can provide a basis for judgment.

According to Tables 2–12 and 2–13, half of the pastors and nearly two-thirds of the seminarians received some kind of academic honor during their undergraduate studies. To the extent that the proportion of students reporting academic honors is higher for each category than it is for pastors, it might be argued that there has been an improvement in the academic achievement of present day seminary students over those of the past.

The tables also suggest that the interdenominational seminaries have attracted a higher proportion of collegiate honor students than any of the other seminary groups. Among seminarians, for example, 76 per cent of those enrolled in the ecumenical seminaries reported having received some type of academic honor, compared with 43 per cent of the students responding from former Evangelical and Reformed schools.

In a related question of a subjective kind, we also asked each respondent to evaluate his undergraduate academic rank in comparison with other members of his college class. In this instance, 47 per cent of the pastors and 61 per cent of the students replied that they ranked "higher than average."

Table 2–12 Undergraduate Academic Honors Received by Pastors (by type of seminary attended).

Academic Honor Received	Total	Per Cent Responding E & R	C C	Ind	Other
Number reporting	1,191	360	257	276	298
Phi Beta Kappa	3	1	2	8	2
Dean's list	36	32	38	44	32
Local honor roll	13	12	11	16	15
Honors courses	11	6	8	19	14
Other	10	9	11	13	10
None reported	49	58	50	35	51

Totals exceed 100 per cent because of multiple choices.

Table 2–13 Undergraduate Academic Honors Received by Seminarians (by type of seminary attended).

Academic Honor Received	Per Cent Responding Total	E & R	C C	Ind
Number reporting	1,283	187	337	759
Phi Beta Kappa	6	1	1	9
Dean's list	48	30	36	58
Local honor roll	16	7	12	19
Honors courses	22	13	16	28
Other	15	9	9	19
None reported	35	57	48	24

Totals exceed 100 per cent because of multiple choices.

When these responses were analyzed by seminary groups, the same pattern we described in the previous question appeared; that is, a higher proportion of those attending interdenominational schools considered their academic standing to be "higher than average" than those attending denominational seminaries.

To summarize our findings in this chapter, ministers of the United Church of Christ are recruited predominantly from urban places and from homes in which the father was employed in a white collar occupation. We found that the ministry as a means of upward social mobility is less salient now than it was in the past.

We have observed that the nurture given by the respondent's local church during his formative years was positively perceived by a large majority of our survey population. The primacy given to the pastor of the respondent's local church in helping him decide on the ministry as a vocation underlines the importance of the pastor's function in recruiting persons for the ministry.

Our findings give support to Browne Barr's observations about the minister as the primary professional role model for the prospective seminarian. In the Introduction to his Lyman Beecher Lectures, Barr wrote: "Most ministers I know, who are professionally content, claim that they did not become ministers, so far as they know, because someone exhorted them to do so, but because somewhere along the line they knew a minister to whom they responded affirmatively."[15]

Finally, men recruited for the ministry of this denomination tend to come out of denominationally related colleges, the large majority of them with undergraduate majors in the Humanities and the Social Sciences. We found that our student respondents as a group were less likely than our group of pastors to have majored in the social sciences as undergraduates; baccalaureate majors in religion appear to be increasing among the present generation of theological students.

3

The Education of the Minister

In the report prepared for the Commission on Theological Education of the United Church of Christ, Paul M. Harrison included an analysis of course listings for the academic year 1965–1966 published by the 13 seminaries in this study. A total of 2,025 courses were listed, averaging 155 courses per seminary. The lowest number of courses was offered by Bangor Theological Seminary (69) and the highest number by Union Theological Seminary (271).

These courses were classified into seven categories and, according to Professor Harrison's computations, were distributed as follows:

Bible	25.69%
History and Theology	27.67
Religion and Society	11.63
Religion and Personality	6.42
Contemporary Culture	2.53
Practical Theology	22.26
History of Religions	3.44

In ten of the thirteen schools, fully three-fourths of all courses were in the traditional fields of theological education:

Bible, History and Theology, and Practical Theology. The most significant deviations from this norm occurred in three fields: Chicago and United seminaries provided proportionately more courses in Religion and Society, Andover Newton and Chicago ranked highest in the number of Religion and Personality courses offered, and Hartford Seminary Foundation provided substantially more courses in History of Religion than any of the other schools. Beyond these distinctions, however, the majority of courses offered by all thirteen seminaries were in the traditional fields mentioned above.[1]

Given these facts, it comes as no surprise that the pastors and seminarians in our survey ranked Biblical and Theological studies first and second as their major fields of study in seminary. As a group, pastors ranked the practical field as third choice, while Ethics and Society was the third most frequently reported major for seminarians. This change reported by presently enrolled students may be an indicator of what some observers characterize as a growing concern for social relevance in the education of ministers. We noted in our first chapter that the second "most pressing" decision personally faced by our respondents had to do with the "nature of my personal involvement in controversial social issues."[2]

The most significant deviation among the various seminary groups is suggested by Professor Harrison's observation that the Congregational Christian seminaries provided the highest proportion of courses in the field of Religion and Personality. According to our survey data, pastors attending these seminaries ranked majors in Religion and Personality ahead of Theology (but behind Bible), while students attending these institutions at the time of the survey ranked Religion and Personality ahead of both Bible and Theology.

Forty-seven per cent of the pastors and 45 per cent of the seminarians majored in Bible or Theology. It is of interest to note in this connection that majors in the third traditional field of theological education, History, declined from 12 per cent for ministers to only 7 per cent for seminarians.

In view of this overwhelmingly traditional structure reflected in the formal curricula of the seminaries, indicators of change in theological education must be sought elsewhere. We shall begin by turning to the need for change as it is expressed by those who are the primary consumers of theological education.

The Need for Change

When the ministers and students were asked to give an overall evaluation of theological education in the United States, only 11 per cent of the pastors and 6 per cent of the seminarians felt that "on the whole, theological education . . . is doing a good job training ministers." More than one-fourth of the ministers and nearly one-third of the students believed that seminary education in the United States "needs to be completely overhauled." Between these extreme positions, the majority of all respondents conceded that the education of ministers "needs some change to keep up with the times."

The most critical judgment—that theological education needs to be completely overhauled—ranged from only 10 per cent of the pastors who attended former Evangelical and Reformed seminaries to 37 per cent of the seminarians currently enrolled in the seven ecumenical schools.

The change anticipated in theological education by some of these critics may be one of degree rather than of kind. An underlying assumption behind major contemporary critiques of American religion is that the church ought to become more relevant to contemporary social issues. For the church to become more socially relevant, it is further assumed that the content of theological education should place greater emphasis on social issues and correspondingly less on the traditional courses taught in the seminaries.

To explore this line of reasoning, we included a question in our survey asking how helpful the individual's seminary experience had been in understanding contemporary social issues. We selected five specific areas of social concern in our question: civil rights, technology, public education, foreign policy, and local community problems.

The results are reported in Tables 3–1 and 3–2. In these tables we combined two categories of responses ("quite adequate" and "fairly adequate") to show the proportion in each group who felt that their seminary education was at least fairly adequate in each area. We find that the majority of the ministers felt that their seminary education was adequate in two of the specified areas—civil rights and local community problems—while most seminarians reported that their professional education was adequate in all areas except public education.

This difference between the responses of pastors and seminarians provides another indicator that theological education in this denomination is becoming more relevant to social issues than it has been in the past.

When corresponding cells in the two tables are compared, in each case a higher percentage of seminarians considered their seminary education to be adequate than did the pastors. Respondents related to former Evangelical and Reformed seminaries were most satisfied with their education in relation to these issues, while those attending former Congregational Christian institutions were most critical. As will be shown later, this difference is a function of different expectations among students enrolled in these two types of seminaries and does not mean that the former provides more social-issue oriented courses than the latter. The attitudes expressed are functions of the educational style of individual seminaries; levels of adequacy reported are relative to what is expected in each seminary. The only inference to be drawn from these tables at this point is that, on the whole, seminarians seem to be fairly satisfied with the way in which contemporary social issues are being dealt with in their theological education; and to the extent that they are more satisfied than their predecessors in school, one might also

Table 3–1 Pastors' Positive Evaluation of Seminary Education and Social Issues (by type of seminary attended).

Social Issue	Per Cent Responding Total	E & R	C C	Ind	Other
Number reporting	1,191	360	257	276	298
Issues and strategy of the civil rights movement	63	72	61	65	51
Problems of automation and technological change	46	58	43	45	35
Issues confronting public education	42	50	36	42	38
Issues and strategy relating to American foreign policy	37	34	32	51	30
Ministers' role in local political, economic, and social structures	55	61	50	57	49

Table 3–2 Seminarians' Positive Evaluation of Seminary Education and Social Issues (by type of seminary attended).

Social Issue	Per Cent Responding Total	E & R	C C	Ind
Number reporting	1,283	187	337	759
Issues and strategy of the civil rights movement	71	86	65	69
Problems of automation and technological change	57	76	54	54
Issues confronting public education	46	58	43	44
Issues and strategy relating to American foreign policy	50	49	43	53
Ministers' role in local political, economic, and social structures	65	76	60	65

infer that theological education in the United Church of Christ is becoming more socially relevant.

The attitudes of respondents toward some of the controversial public issues of our time may provide us with other indicators of the general social-issue orientation of theological education in the denomination. In Tables 3–3 and 3–4 we report responses on three major issues: war, abortion, and divorce. If we assume that the liberalization of traditional

Table 3–3 Pastors' Attitudes toward Controversial Issues (by type of seminary attended).

	Per Cent Responding				
Social Issue	Total	E & R	C C	Ind	Other
Number reporting	1,191	360	257	276	298
Oppose U.S. policy in Vietnam	51	45	50	66	45
Favor liberalized abortion laws	69	56	74	83	68
Favor liberalized divorce laws	43	28	43	61	42

Chi-squares: 46.7292, 67.7054, 86.5128; $df = 9$; $p =$ less than .001.

Table 3–4 Seminarians' Attitudes toward Controversial Issues (by type of seminary attended).

	Per Cent Responding			
Social Issue	Total	E & R	C C	Ind
Number reporting	1,283	187	337	759
Oppose U.S. policy in Vietnam	64	43	60	71
Favor liberalized abortion laws	69	59	62	74
Favor liberalized divorce laws	45	25	38	53

Chi-squares: 59.6309, 26.1369, 90.2052; $df = 6$; $p =$ less than .001.

norms is an expression of "social relevance" (a highly debatable assumption implicit in much of the current rhetorical writing about the church), we find that respondents identified with former Evangelical and Reformed seminaries are least opposed to American policy in Vietnam and least supportive of efforts to liberalize existing divorce and abortion laws, while those related to the interdenominational schools are most opposed to the war and most in favor of liberalizing existing laws.

These tables also confirm what we have described earlier, that the present generation of theological students is moving toward a more liberal position on social issues: in most of the cells in these tables, the proportion responding is higher for seminarians than it is for pastors.

Whatever one's judgment with respect to these specific controversial issues, it is clear that distinctions can be made in terms of the degree of commitment to changes in existing social policies. Another indicator comes from statistics reported in Chapter 5 (Tables 5–6 and 5–7) which describe a variety of experiences reported by our survey groups. We asked, for example, if the respondent had ever marched in a picket line. One fourth of the students enrolled in former Evangelical and Reformed seminaries replied "yes" to this question, in contrast to almost half of those attending the interdenominational schools; seminarians attending former Congregational Christian institutions fell between these extremes, with 36 per cent reporting experience on a picket line.

One final indicator that differentiates styles of theological education in the United Church of Christ is the identification of those issues that were controversial during one's seminary residence. The pastors reported uniformly (regardless of seminary group) that the most controversial issues discussed during their seminary days had to do with "the salience of the parish church" and the "church and the civil rights movement."

Student reports of "very controversial issues" were more differentiating than those of the pastors. Seminarians attending former Evangelical and Reformed schools reported the most controversial issues in the following order: sense of "community," church and the civil rights movement, and the meaning of corporate worship. Students in former Congregational Christian seminaries listed church and the civil rights movement first, followed by the salience of the parish church, and national politics. Interdenominational seminary students listed national politics first, followed closely by sense of "community," and the church and the civil rights movement.

Liberalizing Effect of Theological Education

If the church is the bastion of traditionalism, as some of its critics believe, then one would expect that its educational institutions would be the primary agents for conserving its traditionalism. On the other hand, where the churches are voluntary associations, enjoying no hegemony over other institutions in a free society, and where their educational institutions are equally free of direct ecclesiastical control, prophetic religious leaders can emerge, challenging the traditionalism of both the church and society.

What effect does the education provided by the theological schools affiliated with the United Church of Christ have on the religious and social value commitments of their students? Does the seminary simply reinforce the values which the student brings with him, or are those values changed in any way? Our survey data suggest that, where the views of students are changed, they are changed overwhelmingly in the direction of greater liberalism.

Responses given to two questions concern us here. In the first question, each person was asked, "How much have your political views changed since entering seminary?" Only four per cent of all respondents, both ministers and students, reported that their political views had become more conservative since entering the seminary.

Fifty per cent of the pastors and 47 per cent of the students reported that their political views became more liberal during their seminary years. Pastors and students who attended interdenominational seminaries were most likely to have shifted to a more liberal political position, while those who attended former Congregational Christian schools were least likely to change.

The practical consequences of these differences will be found in Tables 5–4 and 5–5, where we report the political party preferences of our respondents. The overwhelming majority of both pastors and students align themselves politically with the Socialists, Democrats, or liberal Republicans. Only one respondent in five considers himself to be a political conservative of either Democratic or Republican genre.

The liberalizing effect of the seminary on the individual's theological views is equally significant. When asked, "How much have your theological views changed since entering the seminary?" 63 per cent of the pastors and 57 per cent of the seminarians reported that they had become "more liberal." About 15 per cent of these respondents' theological positions became more conservative as a result of seminary experience.

Respondents who attended the Evangelical and Reformed seminaries were more likely to report the liberalizing of their theological views than those who attended other types of schools, while the minority who reported becoming more conservative were likely to have attended Congregational Christian or interdenominational seminaries.

Since the terms "liberal" and "conservative" are relative to particular theological positions, we need now to describe more explicitly the theological views of our respondents. We asked each person to characterize his general theological perspective by identifying himself with a theological "label" and with specific contemporary theologians whose views most closely represented his own. Granting the difficulty of theological labels, we suggested ten possible positions and a space for those who could not identify with any of the positions we listed. The form of our question proved functional for our purposes, since more than 90 per cent of our respondents were able to identify themselves with at least one of the theological labels. Their responses are found in Tables 3–5 and 3–6.

Table 3–5 Theological Perspective of Pastors (by type of seminary attended).

	Per Cent Responding				
Theological Perspective	Total	E & R	C C	Ind	Other
Number reporting	1,191	360	257	276	298
Liberal-theistic	13	8	19	10	18
Neo-orthodox with philosophical emphasis	16	15	18	18	15
Neo-orthodox with Biblical emphasis and radical depravity	12	19	9	7	11
Neo-orthodox with Biblical emphasis and partial depravity	29	38	19	37	19
Biblical conservative	8	5	7	3	18
Biblical fundamentalist	*	*	0	0	1
Thomistic	*	0	0	0	*
Liberal-Humanistic	3	1	4	2	6
New Theology	29	27	35	36	21
Radical Theology	2	2	2	1	2
Other	4	3	5	4	4
None reported	2	3	3	*	2

* less than 0.5 per cent.

(See Table 3–6 below for names of theologians identified with each label.)

Table 3–6 Theological Perspective of Seminarians (by type of seminary attended).

Theological Perspective	Per Cent Responding Total	E & R	C C	Ind
Number reporting	1,283	187	337	759
Liberal-theistic (Brightman, Fosdick, Whitehead, Meland, Hartshorne)	10	9	12	9
Neo-orthodox with philosophical emphasis (Tillich)	18	17	18	18
Neo-orthodox with Biblical emphasis and radical depravity (Brunner, Barth)	11	15	8	12
Neo-orthodox with Biblical emphasis and partial depravity (The Niebuhrs)	24	25	19	25
Biblical conservative (not identified with any particular theologian)	1	0	*	*
Biblical fundamentalist (not identified with any particular theologian)	1	0	*	1
Thomistic (Maritain, Gilson)	1	0	*	1
Liberal-Humanistic (Wieman)	4	2	3	5
New Theology (Bonhoeffer, etc.)	25	32	32	21
Radical Theology (Altizer, etc.)	3	0	4	3
Other	6	1	5	8
None reported	2	5	2	2

The order in which frequencies are reported in these tables is the order in which the "labels" appeared in the questionnaire. The findings are suggestive. To begin, while the majority identified themselves with only one theological position, approximately 15 per cent of the pastors and 5 per cent of the seminarians selected more than one label. In several instances as many as four labels were checked.

One might speculate on the meaning of these multiple choices and the higher frequency of such choices by our group of pastors. The ambivalence suggested by those identifying with more than one position may indicate that their theological views are changing or uncertain. The relatively low rate of multiple choices among students may be attributed to the influence of the dominant views espoused by their theological professors, or a reflection of theological sophistication arising from their daily grappling with theological issues in the classroom.

We examined the pattern of multiple choices by pastors and found that the "New Theology," which we identified with Bonhoeffer, appeared most frequently. For example, 24 per cent of the pastors who identified themselves with Tillich's theological position also identified with Bonhoeffer; 29 per cent of the ministers who identified with Barth and Brunner also selected Bonhoeffer; and 15 per cent of the "Niebuhrians" also selected the New Theology label.

In other words, the multiple selections on the part of the pastors are concentrated among those who identify themselves with the variant forms of the neo-orthodox theological position. To the extent that the New Theology of Bonhoeffer appeared more recently in the discourse of American theological education than those we have identified as Neo-orthodoxy, we would surmise that a number of pastors are moving away from the "older" neo-orthodoxy of the Niebuhrs and Tillich toward the "newer" form represented by Bonhoeffer. For many of the pastors in our survey, the writings of Bonhoeffer did not appear in the theological curriculum until after their professional studies were completed. The higher frequency of multiple choices among pastors may thus be explained as an indicator of theological change, rather than uncertainty or confusion.

Because of these multiple choices, it is not possible to describe the various positions on the theological spectrum in any composite way. What is at once clear is that theological education in the United Church of Christ is marked by theological diversity, rather than uniformity. The range of theological positions taken by our respondents underlines the ecumenical character of this denomination.

However, the majority of all respondents did identify themselves with some variant of the neo-orthodox position. Within this general perspective, adherents of the New Theology of Bonhoeffer and the neo-orthodoxy of the Niebuhrs and Tillich predominated.

The order in which the various viewpoints rank varies from group to group. It is not surprising, for example, that the theology of the Niebuhrs ranked first for pastors who attended former Evangelical and Reformed seminaries and the interdenominational schools. The Niebuhrs were identified with the Evangelical and Reformed Church and spent their academic careers at Yale Divinity School and Union Theological Seminary.

A comparison of Tables 3–5 and 3–6 shows that the liberal-theistic position, which once held a dominant role in American theology, is clearly in the minority now. Among pastors who attended former Congregational Christian seminaries, this position was most salient; the decline in support of this position on the part of currently enrolled seminarians suggests that the liberal theological position is becoming marginal to the denomination's theological scene.

At the time of the survey, a great deal of public attention was being focused on the radical "Death of God" theology of Altizer and others. Our data indicate that this position is of little import to ministers and theological students of this denomination.

Finally, the theological perspectives we have called "Biblical conservatism" and "Biblical fundamentalism" are, for all practical purposes, residual positions for seminarians. While 8 per cent of the pastors identified themselves as Biblical conservatives, the largest proportion holding this position were pastors who were trained in seminaries affiliated with other denominations.

To sum up, the United Church of Christ is characterized by a diversity of theological positions, and these positions are in part a function of the type of seminary in which the minister is educated. Neo-orthodoxy is the dominant theological orientation, particularly the positions articulated by Bonhoeffer, the Niebuhrs, and Tillich. Radical theological positions of the right and left are supported by only a small minority of pastors and seminarians of this denomination.

This diffusion of theological positions among the ministers and theological students of the United Church of Christ is also the consequence of the denomination's refusal to make doctrinal orthodoxy a norm for church membership and ordination. James M. Gustafson's observation in this context is instructive. "The social effect of such tolerance," he wrote, "is often a denomination without consensus, not only about dogma, but also about purposes and ways of work."[3] Whether he is correct or not remains to be seen in our next chapter, where we take up the work of the minister.

The Style of Theological Education

Emerging from our data is the diversity of educational styles in the United Church of Christ. Further evidence for this diversity is found in the assessments made by our respondents of the adequacy of theological education today and their evaluation of optional educational emphases that might be appropriate for the professional education of ministers in the years ahead.

In one of our questions, we listed 16 different ways in which the professional education of ministers might be emphasized. The areas most frequently selected by our survey groups will be discussed in Chapter 4, which deals with the work of the minister. In this chapter we will use the data in a slightly different way, for the differences in responses to certain items provide us with a basis for delineating different styles of theological education that prevail in the United Church of Christ.

Using the chi-square test as a measure of significance, we are able to select those items (from the original list of 16) which discriminate most among the various seminary groupings in the survey. Eight items were selected from the pastors' responses and six from answers given by students, and these are reported in Tables 3–7 and 3–8.

Table 3–7 Educational Emphases to which Pastors Attach Great Importance (by type of seminary attended).

		Per Cent Responding			
Type of Educational Emphasis	Total	E & R	C C	Ind	Other
Number reporting	1,191	360	257	276	298
Extensive knowledge of practical fields such as preaching, Christian education, etc.	50	61	46	34	55
Providing opportunities for active involvement in contemporary social movements	42	43	39	50	35
Learning how to engage effectively in political action groups and to influence legislation	34	31	32	46	30
Being educated in a seminary which is actively related to a major university	29	16	33	42	30
Developing habits of personal piety and religious devotion	29	29	29	23	35
Developing professional or academic expertise in some nonreligious field	21	15	28	29	16
Becoming knowledgeable about the program and structure of one's denomination	13	17	10	4	19
Reading knowledge of Biblical languages (Greek, Hebrew)	9	16	4	5	9

Chi squares = 82.2225, 27.2853, 39.9207, 80.4362, 35.2846, 53.3716, 67.4695, 75.7091; $df = 9$; p = less than .001.

Table 3–8 Educational Emphases to which Seminarians Attach Great Importance (by type of seminary attended).

Type of Educational Emphasis	Per Cent Responding Total	E & R	C C	Ind
Number reporting	1,283	187	337	759
Working with a professional minister who is a trained supervisor in field intern programs	51	61	59	45
Extensive knowledge of practical fields such as preaching, Christian education	38	66	47	27
Being educated in a seminary which is actively related to a major university	37	16	37	43
Extensive knowledge of the classical theological fields	30	21	21	36
Developing communicative skills, such as the use of radio, TV, etc.	25	27	30	23
Becoming knowledgeable about the program and structure of one's denomination	11	14	14	9

Chi-squares = 36.6290, 119.5278, 119.5235, 35.1977, 26.7248, 22.8542; $df = 6$; p = less than .001.

First, we will compare the items listed on the two tables and determine which items are included in one and missing from the other. We find, for example, that items dealing with extensive knowledge of classical theological studies, field intern programs, and the development of communication skills appear in the seminarians' table but are absent from the list for pastors. Conversely, the pastors' table includes five items not included in the students' list: development of personal piety, involvement in social movements, developing expertise in a nonreligious field, knowledge of Biblical languages, and learning how to engage in political action.

Since the items appear in the tables because of their power

to differentiate among the several seminary groupings, the absence of an item means that there is some consensus among the seminary groups for the particular educational emphasis. Thus the development of piety in the education of ministers, while problematic for pastors in the sense that there were significant differences among them, is less of a problem for seminarians. The same can be said for the other four items that did not appear on the students' list.

Second, there are three items that appear in both tables which continue to make distinctions among the several groups of seminaries: knowledge of the practical fields, the seminary's relationship to a major university, and the importance of denominational programs and structures.

Finally, by rearranging the items in both tables according to their "high" and "low" frequencies, distinctive patterns emerge for each of the seminary groups. In making this rearrangement we have used brief labels for each item reported in Tables 3–7 and 3–8 in order to conserve space. For some items, the frequencies apply to both pastors and seminarians (P & S), while for others they apply only to pastors (P) or seminarians (S).

High	*Low*
Evangelical and Reformed Seminaries	
Practical fields (P & S)	University relationship (P & S)
Denominational program (P & S)	Nonreligious expertise (P)
Biblical languages (P)	Classical fields (S)
Field intern program (S)	
Congregational Christian Seminaries	
Denominational program (S)	Biblical languages (P)
Communication skills (S)	Classical fields (S)

High	*Low*
Interdenominational Seminaries	
University relationship (P & S)	Practical fields (P & S)
Classical fields (S)	Denominational program (P & S)
Social movements (P)	Piety and devotion (P)
Nonreligious expertise (P)	Field intern program (S)
Political action (P)	Communication skills (S)
Other Seminaries	
Piety and devotion (P)	Social movements (P)
Denominational program (P)	Political action (P)

We see by the number of items appearing for each seminary group that the greatest degree of dissonance exists between former Evangelical and Reformed schools and the interdenominational schools. As we have observed in other cases, responses of pastors (P) and students (S) associated with former Congregational Christian seminaries more often fall between the two extreme positions.

The appearance of certain items under each seminary group should not surprise us. For example, the denominationally oriented schools were equally high in attaching "great importance" to "becoming knowledgeable about the program and structure of one's denomination," while the interdenominational group ranked this type of educational emphasis low. The interdenominational schools, on the other hand, ranked high the importance of an active relationship with a major university, while this characteristic was given the lowest evaluation by both pastors and seminarians attending the Evangelical and Reformed schools.

We have already noted elsewhere that as a group, pastors and seminarians attending former Evangelical and Reformed seminaries are least preoccupied with thoughts of leaving the ministry for another vocation, feel best equipped to serve as parish ministers, and are most likely to feel that they will remain in the parish ministry after five or ten years. We have also noted that pastors and students identified with the interdenominational institutions are most likely to be thinking of leaving the ministry, are least interested in serving residentially based congregations if they are students, and are least likely to feel that they would be in the parish ministry after five or ten years.

Our analysis of Tables 3–7 and 3–8 provides considerable support for these views. The high priority placed on the practical fields, such as preaching and Christian education, and on well-supervised field internship programs with professional ministers by respondents from the Evangelical and Reformed seminaries, and the correspondingly low priority placed on these educational emphases by respondents from the interdenominational schools, demonstrate the consistency with which these attitudes are expressed.

Pastors who attended the interdenominational seminaries placed their emphases on developing expertise in nonreligious fields of knowledge and in social and political action. For currently enrolled students in these institutions, high priority was also placed on the classical fields of theological education.

These findings are beginning to suggest that there are distinctive styles of theological education within the denomination, and that these styles of education may have consequences for the manner in which the minister defines his work. Let us turn now to the work of the minister and see if the various seminary groups in the United Church of Christ can also be differentiated along this dimension of our study.

4

The Work of the Minister

We began this book with a description of the vocational crisis facing clergymen and students preparing for the ministry. The persistent, if not ubiquitous, conclusion drawn from contemporary studies of the ministry is that there is a confusion about the purpose of the church and its ministry and that this confusion is reflected in a growing disenchantment with the residentially based parish church as the primary locus of the minister's work.

We suggested that the multiplicity of roles demanded of the contemporary minister is not unique to our time and that the anxiety he feels about his professional identity is shared by other professionals. Kenneth Underwood, in reporting the findings of a major study for the Danforth Foundation, makes the following observation which is pertinent to our investigation:

> We are experiencing in theological education at the most basic level a crisis in contemporary religious commitment and consciousness. This crisis is experienced by clergy and laity as multiform contradictions in the thought and action of the churches consciously trying to live with traditional religious faith in a modern technical society. Much in the present situation is not new to other times of crisis: the anguish of doubt in the midst of faith, the temptation

> to wholesale anti-institutional attitudes and to moral nihilism. But today these aspects are expressed in a new setting: a fast-changing, highly specialized, scientifically informed, publicly educated, globally involved society.[1]

Underwood identifies the four "historic modes" of ministry as pastoral, priestly, prophetic-teaching, and governing, and these in turn correspond to four styles or dimensions of professionalism, which he describes as concern for persons, trained skills, values and basic theory, and public responsibility.[2] For professionals to be fully professional, or ministers to be fully ministers, these dimensions must be fully expressed, and it is because the professions have become fragmented through specialization and secularization that we speak of crisis. For the minister, a major consequence of specialization has been "the bias of the minister toward being a man who works with *ideas* and *individuals* rather than with the responsible use of power in the structure of society."[3]

This bias of ministers toward the individual and toward a cognitive style of work is somewhat ambiguously confirmed by our survey data, and it is this ambiguity that points to the uncertainty of the minister's calling. To begin with, in their theological education, both pastors and seminarians were most likely to have majored in Bible, Theology, and Practical Theology in that order of frequency. When asked what seminary courses had been most helpful to them, both groups mentioned courses in Theology and Bible most often, followed by courses in Ethics and Society and Religion and Personality.

In response to the question, "If you had an opportunity for further study, which one of the following fields would be most helpful for your work in the ministry?" 40 per cent of the ministers and 32 per cent of the students selected Psychology, a field most relevant to their pastoral counseling role. The next most frequently mentioned field, Social Science, was a poor second, with only 19 per cent of both groups making this choice.

We have already noted in Table 1–7 that pastors and seminarians ranked "study groups" first in order of importance when asked to evaluate the importance of church programs.

Thus, the predisposition of ministers and of those training to become ministers appears to be strongly in the direction of working with ideas and individuals, rather than with the responsible use of power in the structure of society, as Underwood argued.

However, our data is not entirely consistent, underlining the dilemma faced by clergymen in our time. In another

Table 4–1 Attitudes of Pastors toward New Forms of Theological Education (by type of seminary attended).

Form of Education Considered to be of "Great Importance"	Total	Per Cent Responding E & R	C C	Ind	Other
Number reporting	1,191	360	257	276	298
Ability to analyze contemporary social problems	70	70	68	74	69
Being educated in an ecumenical environment	58	58	58	66	51
Working with a professional minister who is a trained supervisor in field intern programs	56	62	54	58	49
Developing habits of scholarly research and articulate presentation of ideas	54	52	56	57	54
Learning techniques for analyzing the local social situation, including political and economic behavior	53	53	50	60	51
Extensive knowledge of practical fields such as preaching, Christian education, etc.	50	61	46	34	55

Table 4–2 Attitudes of Seminarians toward New Forms of Theological Education (by type of seminary attended).

Form of Education Considered to be of "Great Importance"	Per Cent Responding Total	E & R	C C	Ind
Number reporting	1,283	187	337	759
Ability of analyze contemporary social problems	73	75	76	71
Learning techniques for analyzing the local social situation, including political and economic behavior	58	58	61	57
Being educated in an ecumenical environment	57	58	55	57
Working with a professional minister who is a trained supervisor in field intern programs	51	61	59	45
Developing habits of scholarly research and articulate presentation of ideas	51	46	48	53
Extensive knowledge of practical fields such as preaching, Christian education, etc.	38	66	47	27

question, we asked each respondent to indicate the degree to which he considered selected forms of theological education to be important for the training of future ministers. In Tables 4–1 and 4–2, we report responses for all items in which at least half of the respondents placed "great importance" for theological education.

The original question contained 16 separate items, and for both pastors and seminarians, the same 6 items appear at the highest order of frequency, although the order in which each item appears differs. Both groups placed their highest priority on the importance of the minister's "ability to analyze contemporary social problems." Currently enrolled seminarians ranked second their need for "learning techniques for analyzing the local social situation, including political and economic behavior."

The dilemma of theological education is this: pastors and seminarians are educated in the humanities as undergraduates, concentrate on traditional historical and theological studies during their seminary years, and perceive a need for greater knowledge and competence in the social sciences. Yet, when asked to evaluate the various ways in which they do their work, they place their highest priority on cognitive activities and desire more training in psychology, rather than in the social sciences.

Underwood suggests "the responsible use of power in the structure of society" as the alternative to the bias toward working with ideas and individuals. In this context we note that two of the items at the very bottom of the list for both ministers and students were "becoming knowledgeable about the program and structure of one's denomination," and "learning how to act effectively in ecclesiastical political work." The fact that clergymen place very low priority on the organizational and political dimensions of their own denomination is an indicator of the present crisis in the church and of the church's inability to deal effectively with contemporary social issues.

It is in the denominational form, as distinguished from the parochial form of social organization, that the church manifests its political power. The denominational structure of the church has functions unique to it, just as residentially based congregations have functions they are peculiarly equipped to perform. The function of the denomination is to serve social groups rather than individuals; it is at this level that the church's power can be used responsibly in relation to the structures of society.

The general assemblies of the denomination pass social resolutions which set forth the goals of public policy. Denominational leaders are often called to testify at public hearings, making possible the contribution of the church in the determination of public policy. It is the denominational organization, through its fiscal resources, which provides funding for new and experimental forms of ministry and reallocates the resources from areas of affluence to areas of need. To the extent that changes in the structures of society are basically made through political action, it would appear that the unique role of the denominational organization as an agent of social change needs to be reappraised.

In light of the dilemma we have been describing about the work of the minister, we want to focus on two important aspects of his professional role—administration and pastoral care—which may provide a constructive basis for a new style of ministry. In placing our emphases on these roles we imply no subordination of other roles traditionally applied to the ministry: preaching, teaching, leading worship, or prophetic witness, for all of these roles are integral to his work as administrator and pastor.

Administration and Ministry

For many, the term "administration" is a pejorative when used in describing the work of the minister. James E. Dittes, of Yale Divinity School, recently described the problem as follows:

> Administrative work is the bane of ministry, by most accounts. It is, as ministers often see it, the unwelcome and unmanageable burden they carry that retards the progress of their ministry as they want to pursue it. Ministers report themselves caught in administrative work when they want to be in ministry. When ministers are asked what part of their work they most enjoy or think most important, they mention pastoral, or preaching, or teaching activities first, and administration comes last. But when they are asked how they actually spend their time, administration comes a clear first, and the others lag behind. This is the often replicated finding of research studies.[4]

Professor Dittes' observation is confirmed by our survey, for we have already seen in Table 1–8 that pastors, seminarians, and laymen are all agreed that ministers spend "too much time" on office and administrative work and "too little time" pursuing other activities that are presumably more in keeping with the proper work of clergymen.

In our view, the term "administration," like the term "bureaucracy," is a descriptive rather than a normative category, and properly understood, it can provide a basis for effective and mission-fulfilling ministry.

Ordway Tead, who has written extensively on administrative theory, defines administration as "the necessary activities of those individuals (executives) in an organization who are charged with the ordering, forwarding and facilitating of the associated efforts of a group of persons brought together to realize some defined purpose."[5] While Tead was primarily concerned about the leadership of industrial corporations, his definition is appropriate to religious organizations as well. It is consistent with Underwood's conception of the ministry as "the work not of professional individuals alone but of corporate bodies of persons who are intentional about shaping the forms of human life in society in response to their perceptions of the actions of God in the events of the world."[6]

Whatever else the church may be, it is a deliberate association of people who are banded together to achieve goals they have in common. As a community of believers, pastor and people are better able to achieve certain goals together than through individual action. In order to achieve their common goals, certain administrative tasks are unavoidable. The time, place, and date for meetings must be set, preparation must be made to serve communion, the telephone must be answered, and the parish newsletters must be mimeographed and mailed.

But beyond these routine activities, administrative work also has important consequences for the mission of the church. Congregations must raise money to pay salaries, maintain church properties, and purchase office supplies, but decisions must also be made about contributing to benevolent causes and to the budgets of denominational mission boards. When a congregation or mission board votes to fund a community action project, urges legislative reform, or joins a movement for social justice, the necessary administrative acts take on deeper meaning because they are geared to the goals and aspirations of more inclusive institutions and the larger community. Often, the only effective means a local congregation has to participate in specific causes is through administrative action, such as by conducting a fund-raising campaign to support the work of a mission board or to provide food and medical supplies to victims of disaster at a distant place.

Dittes suggests that much of the minister's antagonism toward administrative work is a form of scapegoating based on irrational prejudice, for the failure of ministry is most often blamed on administration. He argues that "administrative encounters provide a uniquely vital occasion for the fashioning of ministry—be it pastoral, arousal to mission, or whatever—because they are occasions of immediate involvement in which minister and parishioner share a problem together."[7]

If administration is "the bane of ministry" to some, it is "a social undertaking of fundamental public importance" to others. Ordway Tead views administrative skill as one deserving "to be recognized as a *fine art*" for it brings "closer together in purpose the organized relationships of individuals and groups to each other."[8] It may be useful in our analysis of the minister's work to examine his administrative role from Tead's perspective, for administration is not only an accepted role, but one that is esteemed as well.

Tead identifies six "aspects of organization aims" which are the primary concerns of the administrator: legal, functional, technical, profit-making, personal, and public. Let us examine these aspects from Tead's corporate organizational perspective and transpose them for the clergyman as the administrator of an organized church.

The *legal* aims of an organization are those set forth in its charter, constitution, or by-laws which specify the general purpose of the group. The governing body, such as the trustees or directors, addresses itself more closely to conform to these aims than do other members of the organization. It is especially sensitive to the particular laws and regulations that impinge upon the activities of the organization and is responsible for governing the affairs of the group in ways consistent with the legal aims.

A local church, whether or not it is legally incorporated, must fulfill certain legal aims. Normally these would have to do with matters relating to church properties, mortgages, insurance, employment, health and sanitation, and similar matters. The legal responsibilities of the minister and the church board are parallel to those of a corporation's chief executive officer and his board of directors.

For a business corporation, *functional* aims center on the fulfillment of a social need, primarily in meeting the demand for the production of goods and services. According to Tead, the aim of good functioning is "pride in the total corporate effort—in turning out a good product, fairly priced, with favorable consumer reception, and with cordial labor relations."[9]

While religious organizations do not normally produce goods, they do exist to provide services covering a wide range of human needs and aspirations. The manifest functions of the church are most often described by the traditional work of ministry: preaching, teaching, worship, and pastoral care. Churches also perform latent functions, some of which may be inconsistent with their manifest functions and purposes, such as ascribing social status to their members or giving religious sanction to the values and interests of the privileged classes. The administrative task of the minister is to organize his work and the activities of his parishioners to make sure that the functional requirements of the church are being met adequately.

The third aspect of organizational aims is *technical,* referring to the more specialized, planning, and engineering efforts of business organizations to assure the maximum utility of technological equipment and process requirements. The art of administration calls upon the executive to balance technological and humane considerations, particularly when technology threatens to replace large numbers of the working force.

While technology in this sense is applicable mainly to large-scale church organizations, such as a denominational pension board that decides to computerize its accounting procedures, the average clergyman's "technology" is more likely to be in the realm of technical knowledge and skills required to perform his professional tasks. Occupational obsolescence is as likely for the minister as it is for the engineer. The transformation of Biblical knowledge as a result of new scientific discoveries, the development of new skills in pastoral care or group work, the need to be informed about emerging forms of social and political organization, as well as new currents of theological reflection are among the areas in which the minister's "technical" competence must keep pace with the times. This is more than simply a matter of trying to keep up on one's reading after leaving the seminary; it is the minister's need to organize his work and that of his congregation so that continuing education becomes an essential and organized aspect of his work.

While *profit making,* the fourth aspect of organizational aims in Tead's list, is not germane to such voluntary associations as churches, there is an obvious need for churches to be fiscally responsible and to maintain a membership base adequate to sustain itself as an organized group and to meet its functional requirements. Much of the administrative work of the minister focuses on this aspect, and though some may denigrate such tasks, the fact remains that the primary aims of the church, as a group of people banded together to achieve goals they have in common, will have little chance of realization unless the economic requirements of the congregation are taken seriously and met responsibly.

Perhaps one reason why ministers are often reluctant to accord esteem to this aspect of administrative work is because membership and church finance statistics are often used as the primary indicators of the minister's success or failure—just as the profit and loss statement is used to evaluate economic organizations—and they know that ministry and mission cannot be measured in such statistical terms. However, given the institutional nature of the church, such indicators have their appropriate utility and function, and the art of church administration is to keep the financial aspects of the church in proper balance with the less precise, if not more important, indicators of the church's growth and vitality.

As these words are written, the national agencies of the denomination are faced with severe financial stress. When mission boards are asked to reduce their budgets by hundreds of thousands of dollars each year, mission workers must be recalled, needed ministries must be curtailed, and new ministries are immobilized for lack of funding. The consequence is the failure, in a real sense, of the organization's mission and role.

The *personal* aspect of organizational aims is important in understanding the motivating forces of organizations. Tead describes this often neglected fifth aspect as "the desire to be accorded prestige for a job well done, or to have a status of recognized eminence, or to have the reputation for being a conspicuous success in some or all phases of management, or even just to exercise power because ego-maximization is a satisfying experience."[10] These are the administrator's personal objectives.

While this aspect is subject to invidious distortion, most

people undoubtedly have the desire for approval by others, though not necessarily by everyone. The minister may desire the approval or esteem of his fellow clergyman, his denominational leaders, his parishioners, and leaders of his community; even the maverick, while discounting the disapproval of "the establishment," seeks the support and approval of those who share his values and aspirations.

If this personal aspect is important for the corporation executive, it is even more important for the minister who must elicit the support and participation of his parishioners to achieve the goals of the church. One way to assess an administrator's style and purposes is to determine who are the people (or groups) from whom he desires approval. A minister may seek the support of only a small but prestigious group within the congregation; or he may possess that art of administration which enables him to win the approval of many different groups, often with conflicting values and different statuses, within the congregation.

The *public* is the final aspect of organizational aims. The most obvious manifestation of this is the great lengths to which industrial corporations go to influence consumer opinion and to project favorable images of themselves through advertising, contributions, and consumer services. Public sentiment itself has a way of modifying organizational aims, as witnessed by the increasing concern being shown by industry over environmental pollution and automobile safety.

Churches, being organized primarily in parochial units, often fail to recognize their public responsibilities in any direct or systematic way. "Public relations" is something corporations and politicians engage in to attract customers or voters: it is presumably not an appropriate activity for the church, except perhaps at the national levels of church organization. The relationship between the church and the local newspaper is generally limited to notices of meetings or accounts of trivial organizational activities, and rarely does one read a local "religious news item" that is newsworthy for the public at large. If those outside the church consider the activities of the churches to be trivial, it may be because the churches themselves have made little effort to develop their public relationships in a more meaningful way. Public relations can be, in the hands of a minister who takes his administrative tasks seriously, a creative means of evangelism and witness.

To sum up, when the task of the administrator is seen in this many-faceted way, it becomes clear that the minister's administrative role can be a significant instrument of ministry and mission. The minister's participation on committees and boards in the church or community are occasions for enabling the church to exercise its prophetic role. Put another way, the ministry of administration is a ministry to social structures—committees, boards, organizations—in which the minister is called upon to care in a pastoral way for the more impersonal and secondary relationships of his parish and community. These are the places at which "the responsible use of power in the structure of society" are located, for it is through the minister's use of administrative skill in dealing with power groups both within and without the church that the mission of the church can be advanced. His administrative responsibilities, rather than being a source of annoyance, can provide the means to supplement his traditional preference for working with ideas and individuals by making him a more effective and responsible leader in the process of social change.

We take encouragement from some of Professor Dittes' reflections on administration:

> . . . Maybe here, on the administrative fringes of action, there is substantial action, after all. . . . Perhaps the "administrative problem" is integrated with the purposes and strategies of ministry. . . . Perhaps ministers devalue administration because that *is* what they do and do well.[11]

A conference executive, reporting on his three-month sabbatical in a Boston-area seminary, had this to say:

> Lack of organizational savvy is one of the greatest problems in the ministry today, and the same can be said of seminary administration. We don't know how to relate persons in structures that release their creative skills and powers, and relate those of coworkers so that the whole team moves together with effectiveness, in an environment that turns people on. What we need is schooling in institutional dynamics, organizational development, planning and organizing for change, goal setting, the creative use of conflict, and the like.
>
> Some savvy in this area would help not only to build genuine community in seminaries; but once built, seminary communities would become models of how Christian community is designed into a structure that enables jobs to be done effectively while helping persons to grow in the bargain. . . .[12]

In discussing the minister's administrative role as we have, we are not implying any kind of priority over other roles, and particularly over those roles relating to his work with ideas and individuals. Our intention is to recover, if possible, an understanding of administration as both functional and necessary for the ministry; for the church, if it is to be faithful to its mission, must address itself not only to primary relationships as individuals and members of nuclear families, but to secondary relationships as members of social groups. Most of the issues relating to social justice that concern pastor and people are in the realm of secondary relationships, for they have to do with how power is organized and distributed in society. It is one thing for the minister to preach an inspiring sermon on social justice; it is the same preacher as artful administrator who is able to organize his congregation for action, who engages himself on committees and works with organizations, who becomes knowledgeable about laws and legal institutions, who takes time to inform himself about the technical aspects of social changes, and who will in the end find fulfillment in his ministry.

Let us turn now to the more personal and primary relationship between the pastor and his people: our second focus on the work of the minister, pastoral care.

Pastoral Care and Ministry

In a nationwide survey of a sample of parishioners of the United Church of Christ, we described the pattern of church participation in our recent volume *The Fragmented Layman*. We summarized the views of more than 8,500 laymen and their church participation in the following way:

> When the participants in [*The Fragmented Layman*] study "look at the church," they tend to give a picture of a group of "church supporters" who are seeking personal help in a general area of faith and devotion. They are a group that appears to be quite contented with what they are receiving from the congregation to which they belong, and they do not wish to have the church become too involved in any specific area of "outreach" or public policy.[13]

In that study, when laymen were asked what reasons were most important to them for joining the church, most frequently mentioned was "for the sake of my children." When asked what kinds of help they wanted most from their church, the following were mentioned most often in order of frequency:

1. Strengthen my faith and religious devotion;
2. Build good moral foundations for my personal life;
3. Raise my children properly.

The modal style of church participation which emerged in that study was one in which the church ministered primarily to the personal and familial needs of the parishioner, to what Gibson Winter referred to as the "privatized sector," as distinguished from the "public" sector.[14]

Earlier in this chapter we observed that the pastors and seminarians in the present survey appeared ambivalent about their style of ministry. When asked how important various types of church programs were, they ranked cognitive and action programs first (that is, study groups, social action groups); when asked what forms of theological education were considered to be of great importance for the training of future ministers, courses dealing with the analyses of social and political issues ranked first. Yet, when asked about specific fields in which they would like to pursue more academic work, courses in Psychology were chosen twice as frequently as courses in the Social Sciences.

This ambivalence is seen further in responses to a question which asked, "What type of ministry do you feel you are best

Table 4–3 Type of Ministry Pastors Feel Best Equipped to Serve (by type of seminary attended).

		Per Cent Responding			
Type of Ministry	Total	E & R	C C	Ind	Other
Number reporting	1,191	360	257	276	298
Parish pastor	66	76	64	55	65
Minister of Christian Education	7	7	9	8	5
Campus minister	7	3	8	13	7
College or seminary teacher	11	6	9	17	12
Minister of Music	1	1	0	1	1
Denominational worker	4	4	5	4	4
Ecumenical worker	6	5	5	9	7
Military chaplain	2	2	3	1	3
Institutional chaplain	4	3	6	4	3
Foreign missionary	2	2	1	1	3
Specialized home missionary	5	3	4	7	5
Other	6	5	6	7	6
None reported	1	1	–	1	2

Table 4–4 Type of Ministry Seminarians Feel Best Equipped to Serve (by type of seminary attended).

Type of Ministry	Per Cent Responding Total	E & R	C C	Ind
Number reporting	1,283	187	337	759
Parish pastor	45	72	53	34
Minister of Christian Education	7	10	11	5
Campus minister	7	2	8	8
College or seminary teacher	25	7	12	36
Minister of Music	1	1	0	1
Denominational worker	1	0	1	1
Ecumenical worker	2	1	2	3
Military chaplain	1	1	1	1
Institutional chaplain	3	2	7	2
Foreign missionary	2	1	1	2
Specialized home missionary	4	2	4	4
Other	7	4	7	7
None reported	5	5	4	5

equipped to serve?" Although two-thirds of the pastors and 45 per cent of the students selected "parish pastor" for their response, distinctions among the various seminary groupings suggest that the ambivalence is not as universal as the data may at first indicate.

Tables 4–3 and 4–4 show that for all groups of respondents, except seminarians enrolled in the interdenominational schools, the majority believe that they are best equipped to serve as parish pastors. Pastors and students attending former Evangelical and Reformed seminaries are not only most predisposed toward the pastoral ministry, but their second choice is also related to work in the parish church as ministers of Christian education.

By contrast, the second most frequently selected type of

ministry for respondents from former Congregational Christian seminaries and schools of other denominations is college or seminary teaching. The greatest variance is shown by the preferences of students enrolled in the ecumenical schools: the larger proportion of them (36 per cent) feel they are best equipped for teaching and only secondarily for the pastoral ministry.

Also of interest in these tables is that paraparochial or nonparochial forms of ministry, except for teaching, are possibilities for only a small proportion of our respondents. This suggests that the seminaries have done little thus far in training men for other than the pastoral or teaching ministry.

For most of our respondent groups, the evidence is heavily weighted on the side of the parish ministry. Ministers are primarily trained for this role, they seek additional training to better equip themselves in pastoral care, and their parishioners join their churches primarily to be ministered to in traditional ways. Caring for the spiritual and moral welfare of individuals and families is what pastors do and do well; the church remains preeminent among social organizations equipped to serve people in this way.

Yet we have noted a significant degree of disenchantment with the pastoral ministry. For two-thirds of our respondents, the idea of leaving the ministry for some other vocation continues to have some appeal. By training, most are not sufficiently equipped to enter another profession, including the teaching profession. Even when nonparochial forms of ministry are suggested, such as entering specialized ministries or becoming denominational or ecumenical workers, only a handful feel themselves to be prepared.

In reflecting on the dilemma that emerges from our data, we would venture a possible interpretation. The decade of the 60s has been one in which all of our major institutions have been challenged in unprecedented ways. In our judgment, one of the most persuasive critics of the church early in that decade was Gibson Winter, whose book, *The Subur-*

ban Captivity of the Churches, in 1961 anticipated the issues that were to shake the churches from the complacency they enjoyed during the preceding decade. Professor Winter described the "new style of Protestantism" as one characterized by " (1) an exodus to the suburbs, (2) the identification of Protestantism with the new middle class, and (3) the adoption of an organizational style of religious community in place of the representative congregation."[15] The churches, as a consequence, became "introverted," leading him to the following conclusion:

> The disengagement of the churches from responsibility for the metropolitan community came about as a consequence of social change; the neighborhood and residential area became a private sphere of life in an industrial society, yet religious congregations continued to center their memberships in this private residential sphere. The net effect was to insulate the churches within a privatized sphere—thus disengaging them from public responsibility.[16]

Winter's criticism found considerable support, particularly on the part of church leaders who were beginning to feel guilty about the preoccupation of denominations with suburban church extension during the years following World War II and the obvious neglect of the central cities. The rising protest of the civil rights movement, the war on poverty, and campus and urban disorder turned the churches from institutional aggrandizement to social-issues oriented ministries, particularly among the powerless and disadvantaged. Gradually, denominational home-mission societies began to shift their budgetary allocations from suburban church extension to the inner city; new forms of ministry began to emerge in an effort to make the church more "relevant" to the urgent social problems facing society.

During the past decade, the churches generated their own share of rhetoric and self-criticism, for religion was more a source of comfort than of challenge, and their racism and systematic neglect of the disadvantaged could no longer be rationalized. Suburban ministers in particular were forced into defensive postures or left more affluent congregations for the inner city. "Relevance" and "renewal" become the key concepts, and "new forms of ministry" became the new preoccupation. A number of clergymen, despairing of the dominant form of the church, dropped out of the parish ministry and went to work in social reform movements and social welfare agencies working directly with the disadvantaged. In a recent study of *Ex-Pastors* of the United Church of Christ, Gerald J. Jud and his collaborators reported that 43.5 per cent of those who dropped out of the ministry placed high importance on "Disillusioned with the church's relevance to problems of the modern world" as a reason.[17] The disinterest expressed by a significant portion of today's seminarians in serving the residentially based congregation must be understood in terms of this mood.

However, church administrators who are responsible for funding new forms of ministry, particularly paraparochial and nonparochial ministries which have little promise of achieving self-support, argue that unless these traditional, residentially based parishes continue to grow, there is little chance for the church to be relevant to the pressing needs of society. However one may characterize the more affluent suburban churches, they continue to be the major source of contributions to denominational budgets that support the new ministries. Denominational executives must constantly weigh their decisions against the need for courageous new forms of ministry on the one hand, and the possibility of alienating and cutting off support from more conventional sources on the other.

This theme will be taken up in greater detail in Chapter 5, where we describe the gap that exists between pulpit and pew over social issues. The problem was illustrated recently in a "Letter from an Angry Episcopalian" published in *New York* magazine. The writer is a layman who is a member of a rural mission in Orange County in upstate New York. He took issue with a recent proposal by the Episcopal Diocese of New York which proposed a new system of funding for "outreach in stress areas." The following is a pertinent portion of his letter:

> . . . "Outreach in stress areas" does not stand for the gospel and sacraments of Christ. It does not stand for pastoral work with Christian congregations. It does stand for such things (many of them worthy) as aid to women's lib, the peace movement, the Abortion in Every Pot Committee, radical artistic experiments with the Eucharist and, oddly enough, for a very special emphasis on the legalization of homosexuality. Nothing wrong with any of this in philisophy, but not exactly what the vast majority of Episcopalians envision when they seek for their families "the peace of God which passeth all understanding." It's not charitable or love-filled or "outreaching." It's rank, sensationalist politics. You'd think the leaders of New York Diocese were running for student council seats at Berkeley or Columbia.[18]

Obviously the church must make room for both types of ministry—residentially based parishes and nonparochial "new forms"—without subordinating one type under the other or ascribing a higher degree of "relevance" to one over the other. When people join churches "for the sake of my children," or to seek help "in building good moral foundations," or for "strengthening family relationships," the need for the church's ministry is no less authentic than when others turn to it seeking justice or release from deprivation. The fault has been that the issue is too often defined in "either/or" terms—"Either make your ministry relevant to the major social issues of our time, or get out of the ministry"—rather than seeing the task as one relevant to both social issues and the needs of individuals and their families (who may or may not be socially deprived).

This seemingly conservative assessment is based on assumptions we hold about how justice is to be achieved in our society. We do not believe it will come about solely through appeals to individual conscience or by funding worthwhile paraparochial ministries in areas of human stress, though these activities are both necessary and useful. We agree with Reinhold Niebuhr's observations of many years' standing that social injustices are the consequences of disproportionate power among social groups and that the solution to problems of social conflict must be found in the political sphere.[19]

The residentially based, nuclear-family oriented, and socially stratified parish church is hardly organized for political purposes. Nor are the ministers who serve them trained primarily as social reformers. If religious groups are to deal effectively with problems of injustice in society, appropriate forms of power must be organized for this purpose. This the churches have attempted to do in recent years through their paraparochial forms of ministry, such as the Interreligious Foundation for Community Organization and coalitions formed with such civil rights organizations as the National Welfare Rights Organization and the Southern Christian Leadership Conference.

What we are saying is that the "comforting" role of the church need not be denigrated for the sake of "challenging" the church. We have tried to show, on the basis of our data, that the church is well equipped to serve the comforting role in the context of the residentially based church; we have also tried to suggest that the parish church is a necessary support for the larger church in its ministry of challenge.

In describing the work of the minister in this chapter, we have obviously neglected several important roles traditionally identified with his calling. His roles as preacher, priest, and teacher are not only functionally specific to his profession, they are also roles for which he is systematically trained and about which there is less uncertainty. Our analysis of the minister's work is not intended to be comprehensive, for the concern of this study is with the transitional aspects of the ministry, and we have concentrated on his administrative and pastoral roles as a way to focus on our central problem.

5

The Gap between Pulpit and Pew

In 1963 Pierre Berton, a journalist, was asked to prepare a Lenten reading book for the Anglican Church of Canada. The result was the publication two years later of *The Comfortable Pew,* a lively and often irreverent criticism of the contemporary church. He described the distance that prevailed between the church and the secular world on such topics as civil rights, war and peace, sexual behavior, and business practices and concluded that the church functioned primarily to give comfort to those who found the cares of secular society to be too oppressive. "Institutional Christianity," he concluded, "has become a comfortable creed, a useful tool for Peace of Mind and Positive Thinking, a kind of sugar-coated pill that soothes those who fear to face the traditional Christian concerns of evil, suffering and death."[1]

Shortly thereafter, an empirical study of the "comfort hypothesis" was reported by Charles Y. Glock, Benjamin B. Ringer, and Earl R. Babbie in their volume, *To Comfort and To Challenge,* a portrait of the clergy and parishioners of the Protestant Episcopal Church. These researchers made the following observations of their use of the "comfort hypothesis" to explain one's involvement in parish activities:

> . . . Parishioners whose life situations most deprive them of satisfaction and fulfillment in the secular society turn to the church for comfort and substitute rewards. This is most clearly seen in the case of the two extreme types on the predisposition index. On the one hand, the upper class young father is the darling of our society. His life situation represents much that is considered ideal. He is afforded access to valued achievements and, in turn, is granted greater rewards. As [the tables] show, he is hardly involved in the church at all. At the other extreme, the older lower class spinster enjoys little that would be considered ideal in terms of predominant secular values. Her inability to participate fully and meaningfully in the secular society results in a far greater involvement in church life.[2]

The distinction made by these writers between "comfort" and "challenge" has sound analogues in sociological and theological literature. One thinks first of Max Weber's dichotomy of "priestly" religion and "prophetic" religion. The former is oriented to the social class interests of the ruling group and provides sanctions for the status quo; the latter is concerned with man's relation to the world from an ultimate value position; it stands apart from and is critical of the world.[3]

Another is Ernst Troeltsch's well-known distinction between "church-type" and "sect-type" churches. Membership in church-type churches is socially obligatory; status is ascribed, and the interests of church members are closely allied with national economic and cultural interests. Membership in sect-type churches is voluntary; status is achieved, with emphasis placed on rigorous ethical demands, and the interests of the sects are generally in conflict with those of the nation.[4]

During the past decade a number of writers have criticized the contemporary church for its failure to challenge its parishioners and to engage them more actively in the major social issues of the day. They include Martin Marty, Peter L. Berger, Gibson Winter, and Harvey Cox, to mention the more prominent among them.[5] The general conclusion one draws from the writings of these critics of American religion is that the churches are overwhelmingly committed to the religion of comfort rather than of challenge, that they give "church-type" support to the values and institutions of the privileged rather than take up the "sectarian" cause of the powerless and deprived, and that they are more concerned with the survival of institutional priestcraft than with listening to the discomfiting voice of the prophet.

More recently Jeffrey K. Hadden, a sociologist, has described "the widening gap between clergy and laymen" in his volume, *The Gathering Storm in the Churches.* His central thesis is that "the Protestant churches are involved in a deep and entangling crisis which in the years ahead may seriously disrupt or alter the very nature of the church." He identifies the "crisis" along two dimensions: "a struggle over the very *purpose* and *meaning* of the church," and "a crisis of *belief*"—which in turn have led to "a struggle over *authority*" and "a crisis of identity for the Protestant clergyman."[6]

According to Hadden, the crisis in belief has served to turn the clergyman's emphasis "away from the next world to a deeper concern about the meaning and implications of the Christian faith for this world." In his opinion, "Today, a substantial proportion of the pulpits in American Protestanism are filled by clergymen who hope to see the church become more vitally involved in the world."[7]

The crisis in belief had the opposite consequence for the laity. "Religion [for the laity] has become more privatized. . . . For them, the church is a source of comfort in a troubled world . . . the church is not an agent of change, but rather a buffer against it." This leads Hadden to his final conclusion: "The result is that clergy and laity are on a collision course. In a very real sense, the laity have one church and the clergy have another."[8]

Since the survey data for this study of theological education in the United Church of Christ was collected shortly after we completed our survey for *The Fragmented Layman,* we are in a position to test Hadden's conclusions, for many of the same questions were included in both research projects. Like Hadden, we also centered on issues relating to the civil rights movement to measure the distance that prevails between pulpit and pew over contemporary social issues. We turn now to this task.

Attitudes on Social Issues

As a denomination, the United Church of Christ can be characterized as being liberally oriented toward social issues. During the nineteenth century, Congregationalists in the North provided significant leadership to the movement for the abolition of slavery, and in the years following the Civil War they pioneered in the establishment of educational institutions for freedmen in the South. While some of the church's social pronouncements in the past may appear to be less than liberal from today's perspective, its position on race has kept ahead of existing attitudes and practices.

Through its General Synod resolutions and the activities of its national agencies and local churches, the denomination has been deeply involved in the civil rights movement. In recent years it has participated in the formation of such organizations as the Interreligious Foundation for Community Organization and the Black Economic Development Conference and has supported with funds and staff assistance the National Welfare Rights Organization and the United Farm Workers Organizing Committee. If we were to give sociological content to the norms of social justice prevailing in the United Church of Christ, they would be given in these specific terms.

Hadden, in the study cited above, came to the following "unambiguous" conclusion when he examined the views of clergymen and laymen about issues in the civil rights movement:

> . . . Clergy are extremely sympathetic with the civil rights cause. . . . Laity, on the other hand, are much less committed to implementing integration in American society. . . . the large majority oppose [clergy involvement in the civil rights struggle]. . . .
>
> The implications of these findings should be fairly clear. Conflict between clergy and laity in recent years over the civil rights issue is deeply rooted in fundamentally different views about civil rights and the role that the church and clergy should be playing in this struggle. What is perhaps surprising is that the overt conflict has not been even more serious.[9]

Our studies of the clergy and laity of the United Church of Christ do not lead to Hadden's "unambiguous" conclusion. First, let us compare the attitudes of the laity, as reported in *The Fragmented Layman,* with those of pastors and seminarians in our present study.[10] Three of the major legislative goals of the civil rights movement have been to enact federal laws in the areas of education, employment, and housing. In Table 5–1 we report the percentage of re-

Table 5–1 Attitudes toward Federal Civil Rights Legislation.

Type of Federal Legislation	Per Cent who Favor Laymen	Pastors	Seminarians
Number reporting	8,549	1,191	1,283
Federal aid to public and private education	39	55	65
Federal nondiscriminatory employment legislation	55	93	94
Federal nondiscriminatory housing legislation	44	88	88

spondents among laymen, pastors, and seminarians who favored legislation in these areas.

While federal aid to education is not directly a "civil rights" issue, it is indirectly so to the degree that disadvantaged students have greater opportunities for quality education with federal aid than without it. In Table 5–1 we find seminarians to be most supportive of federal aid to education. While the majority of the pastors support this legislative goal, only 39 per cent of the laity are in favor of it.

On federal legislation dealing with employment and housing, there is no difference between pastors and seminary students. However, the support given by the laymen in the denomination lags far behind, particularly on the issue of nondiscriminatory housing laws.

Since this survey was conducted, the Congress of the United States enacted federal statutes to invalidate discrimination in employment and housing, and in June, 1971, the Supreme Court invalidated certain forms of state aid to parochial schools.

On more specific attitudinal questions, the differences in attitude between laymen, pastors, and seminarians become more explicit. In Table 5–2 we report the proportion in each group who agreed with a number of statements often made in public discussion about civil rights.

Except for the statement concerning property values, there is a remarkable similarity between the responses given by pastors and those given by seminary students. These attitudes are also consistent with the way in which black parishioners of the United Church of Christ responded in the laymen's study.

However, on practically every statement listed in Table 5–2, the attitude of the laymen is consistently opposite that of pastors and seminarians. Clearly, a significant gap exists between the pulpit and the pew as far as specific issues raised by the civil rights movement are concerned.

In another question, we wanted to learn what kind of ac-

Table 5–2 Attitudes Toward Issues in the Civil Rights Discussion.

Statement	Per Cent who Agree Laymen	Pastors	Seminarians
Number reporting	8,549	1,191	1,283
Negroes are trying to move too fast to obtain justice and equality.	51	7	6
Restaurant owners have a right to refuse service to a person because of his race.	22	3	3
When Negroes move into white residential areas, property values tend to go down.	63	17	33
Negroes should be given jobs in proportion to their number in the population.	16	17	22
Negroes are happier in Negro churches and Negro schools.	47	9	10
On the whole, Negro children receive inferior education in comparison to white children.	51	89	89
Negro leaders today are working for the eventual mixture of races through intermarriage.	18	3	3
The Negro is right in demanding his full civil rights now.	56	89	89
We owe the Negro some kind of compensation for past injustices.	17	35	40
Negroes should be hired even if they are not fully qualified, to make up for discrimination against them in the past.	4	10	16

tion was considered most appropriate for the church to take in response to the crisis in race relations. Six possible strategies were suggested, and each person was asked to select the strategy he deemed most appropriate. The results of this question are reported in Table 5–3.

The clergymen and theological students of this denomina-

Table 5–3 Appropriate Church Response to Crisis in Race Relations.

Type of Church Response	Per Cent Responding Laymen	Pastors	Seminarians
Number reporting	8,549	1,191	1,283
The church should not be involved directly.	32	2	1
The church should move no faster on the question than does the neighborhood in which it is located.	39	2	1
The church should deal with the question only in sermons and/or study groups.	22	2	1
Individuals may work on special projects in this area but the church should not involve itself directly.	31	4	4
The church should form a special action group to work on projects dealing with the crisis.	37	28	27
The church should be the leader in the area of race relations.	42	70	71
No response	5	1	1

tion are united in their commitment to the notion that the church should exercise leadership and action in the racial crisis. The attitudes of the laymen are, by contrast, clearly fragmented, ranging from noninvolvement to active leadership. The table also shows that a large proportion of the laymen selected more than one type of church response, indicating an ambivalence about their position on this question.

In reflecting on the meaning of this table we suggest there is a significant flaw in the wall of separation we have been describing between the pulpit and the pew on the civil rights issue. In view of the fact that the laity expresses no real consensus about the church's appropriate role, and that most of the alternatives presented appear to be equally acceptable, one might conclude that the attitudes of the laity are changing. The direction of the change, of course, cannot be determined with certainty, but given the supportive position taken by the denomination in its official pronouncements, and the cohesiveness of the clergy's position, a movement toward greater acceptance is more likely than a movement away from it.

We conclude that the position of the laity on civil rights is at best ambiguous. We fail to see a "collision course," which Hadden attributes to his data, for there is no polarization of attitudes as far as the action of the church is concerned. However, there is substantial disagreement about specific issues concerning the goals of the civil rights movement, but the majority of the laymen (58 per cent) believe that "Churches should support the Negro's struggle to achieve civil rights," and a larger majority (72 per cent) agree that "Ministers have a right to preach on controversial subjects from the pulpit."

Social Action and Involvement

It is one thing to describe the attitudes held by our respondents on controversial social issues; it is quite another to describe one's actual involvement in social action. Unfortunately, comparable data was not collected in our study of the laity, so we will confine our discussion to the kinds of involvement reported by clergymen and students.

On the basis of the attitudes on civil rights that we have attributed to our respondents, we should expect a strong predisposition on their part toward liberal political groups. We asked the ministers and seminary students to indicate their political party preferences along a spectrum ranging from socialists to ultraconservatives. Each category we listed was identified with names of well-known political leaders to give clarity to the label.[11] The results of the political preferences are reported in Tables 5–4 and 5–5.

According to these tables, half of the pastors and seminarians expressed a preference for the Democratic party or leaned in that direction, while one respondent in five expressed a preference for "Liberal Republicans" such as Governor Rockefeller and Senator Javits of New York. If we add to these the small group who preferred the Socialist party and the almost total rejection of conservatives of either party, we find that our respondents are overwhelmingly predisposed toward the liberal position in American politics.

When seminary groups are compared with each other, some differences become apparent. As a group, students and pastors from the interdenominational seminaries are more likely to identify themselves with liberal political positions than those from the denominational schools.

When responses of pastors and students are compared,

Table 5–4 Political Party Preferences of Pastors (by type of seminary attended).

		Per Cent Responding			
Political Party Preference	Total	E & R	C C	Ind	Other
Number reporting	1,191	360	257	276	298
Socialist	4	2	2	7	4
Liberal Democrat	35	35	32	43	28
Conservative Democrat	*	1	*	*	*
Independent-toward Democrat	18	18	17	17	18
Independent-toward Republican	16	17	19	10	19
Liberal Republican	19	20	21	18	19
Conservative Republican	4	3	5	1	8
Ultraconservative	0	0	0	0	0
Other	4	5	4	4	4

* less than 0.5 per cent.
Chi-square = 52.0285; $df = 18$; $p =$ less than .001.
(See Table 5–5 for political leaders identified with each label.)

Table 5–5 Political Party Preferences of Seminarians (by type of seminary attended).

Political Party Preference	Per Cent Responding Total	E & R	C C	Ind
Number reporting	1,283	187	337	759
Socialist (Norman Thomas, etc.)	8	1	9	9
Liberal Democrat (Kennedy, Humphrey, etc.)	32	29	18	39
Conservative Democrat (Russell, Long, etc.)	1	1	2	*
Independent-toward Democrat	17	19	19	16
Independent-toward Republican	14	24	20	9
Liberal Republican (Rockefeller, Javits, etc.)	19	20	21	18
Conservative Republican (Goldwater, Reagan)	3	4	4	2
Ultraconservative (Robert Welch, etc.)	0	0	0	0
Other	6	3	8	7

Chi square = 92.7034; $df = 12$; p = less than .001.

some shift in political party perference is suggested. For both Evangelical and Reformed and Congregational Christian seminaries, a higher proportion of the pastors than of the students identified with the Democrats. Students now enrolled in former Evangelical and Reformed seminaries seem to be shifting toward the Republican party, while students enrolled in former Congregational Christian schools seem to be moving in the direction of the Socialists.

We noted in Chapter 3 that 50 per cent of the pastors and 47 per cent of the students reported that their political views had become more liberal during their seminary years. Only 4 per cent of both groups reported that their political views changed toward a more conservative position during their period of theological education.

In order to describe the respondent's degree of "activism," or involvement in social issues, we asked whether or not the individual had ever participated in a number of different activities. The list of activities included such disparate items as having served in the armed forces, belonged to a labor union, marched in a picket line, or arrested for civil disobedience. One intent of the question was to discover the range of contacts pastors and seminarians had "in the world" and the degree of their involvement in particular kinds of activity outside the church. These responses are recorded in Tables 5–6 and 5–7.

On approximately half the items in these tables there is

Table 5–6 Selected Experiences Reported by Pastors (by type of seminary attended).

	Per Cent Reporting				
Type of Experience	Total	E & R	C C	Ind	Other
Number reporting	1,191	360	257	276	298
Served in the armed forces	32	26	35	30	37
Belonged to a labor union	34	40	30	27	36
Marched in a picket line	35	29	33	51	28
Arrested for "civil disobedience"	3	1	4	5	2
Belonged to a political club	27	18	33	31	27
Undergone psychoanalysis or therapy	27	18	29	32	33
Belonged to a social fraternity	44	36	48	48	45
Lived in racially integrated neighborhood	56	47	57	65	58
Lived on a farm	38	41	34	31	46
Contributed to civil rights group	78	79	79	87	68
Met the mayor	79	78	80	78	82
Met the congressman	68	62	73	66	73
Traveled abroad	46	38	44	57	48

Table 5–7 Selected Experiences Reported by Seminarians (by type of seminary attended).

Type of Experience	Per Cent Reporting Total	E & R	C C	Ind
Number reporting	1,283	187	337	759
Served in the armed forces	14	15	20	11
Belonged to a labor union	22	35	24	19
Marched in a picket line	41	24	36	48
Arrested for "civil disobedience"	3	2	4	3
Belonged to a political club	32	26	31	34
Undergone psychoanalysis or therapy	25	26	31	21
Belonged to a social fraternity	44	41	44	45
Lived in racially integrated neighborhood	56	40	55	60
Lived on a farm	37	40	37	36
Contributed to a civil rights group	68	66	68	69
Met the mayor	49	63	50	46
Met the congressman	49	53	48	48
Traveled abroad	46	38	39	50

almost no difference in the responses from pastors and seminarians. While a slightly higher proportion of students reported having "marched in a picket line," the same proportion carried their protest to the point of being arrested. Equal proportions of both groups have undergone psychoanalysis, belonged to a social fraternity, lived in a racially integrated neighborhood or on a farm, and traveled abroad.

The generational gap was most evident at two points: service in the armed forces and membership in labor unions. Nearly one-third of the pastors had served in the armed forces, in contrast with only 14 per cent of the students; over one-third of the ministers had also been members of labor unions, compared with 22 per cent of the seminary students.

In these tables, the most meaningful indicators of "activism" on social issues are marching in a picket line, being arrested for civil disobedience, and belonging to a political club. As a group, seminarians scored higher than pastors on two of these indicators—a larger proportion of them have marched on picket lines and belonged to political clubs—while only 3 per cent of both groups reported having been arrested for their protest activities.

When these data are examined in terms of the seminary background of the respondent, those who attended interdenominational seminaries were most likely to be activists and those identified with former Evangelical and Reformed schools least active, with respondents from former Congregational Christian institutions occupying an intermediate position. For example, among our students, 48 per cent of those from interdenominational seminaries reported having marched in a picket line, in contrast to 24 per cent of those attending the Evangelical and Reformed schools, a ratio of 2 to 1. One-third of the former group belonged to political clubs, compared with one-fourth of the latter. While the experience of being arrested for civil disobedience was reported by only a small number of men, the same contrasts hold for this item.

The tables show a significant degree of "activism" among ministers and seminarians, but only about one-third of the respondents can be characterized as social activists. To the extent that there are more indicators of student activism than clergy activism, one might expect ministers in the future to be more directly involved in social protest. We do not believe this would necessarily follow, since attitudes toward issues in the civil rights movement are quite similar for both groups. Unlike pastors, who are directly responsible to congregations which pay their salaries and support their work, student activists are not threatened by economic or social "reprisals" should their political activities prove to be unpopular.

There is one final indicator of social action and involvement we would like to report. In this instance, we were able to collect comparable data from our study of the laity. In Table 5–8 we show the percentage of respondents who are *currently* involved in a selected group of nonchurch organizations.

As a group, students are least involved in organizational activities outside the church, and ministers are most involved.

Table 5–8 Current Involvement in Nonchurch Organizations.

	Per Cent who Belong		
Type of Nonchurch Organization	Laymen	Pastors	Seminarians
Number reporting	8,549	1,191	1,283
Charitable or social service	17	34	14
Civil rights group	2	22	16
Community or neighborhood organization	20	38	12
Labor or farmers' union	7	3	3
Political party organization	11	14	14
School or education group	31	31	10
Service or civic group	11	25	6
No nonchurch involvement	23	13	37

While approximately 30 per cent of the pastors and seminarians reported that they had "belonged to a political club" (Tables 5–6 and 5–7), only 14 per cent of both groups were actually participating in these clubs at the time of the survey. Only a minority of all respondent groups are involved in any of the organizations outside the church included in our list. Laymen are most likely to be involved in such school organizations as the P.T.A., while clergymen tend to favor community-oriented groups outside the church.

Style of Ministry and Church Program

The prevailing popularity of Hadden's thesis about "the gathering storm in the churches" obscures what is more fundamental about the gap between the pulpit and the pew. We have shown that while ministers are overwhelmingly in favor of civil rights, their laymen exhibit no consensus, for or against. There is no evidence of polarization between pastor and people; we find little evidence that pulpit and pew are on a "collision course."

The real gap between clergy and laity is to be found in how the two groups define the purpose of the church and its ministry. It is our thesis that both the uncertainty of the minister's calling and the layman's sense of alienation are rooted in their different conceptions of the minister's work and the content of the church's program. All other issues, including the conflict over specific social issues, are derived from this source.

The data used to support this thesis have already been reported in Chapter 1 (Tables 1–7 and 1–8) and will not be repeated here. In Table 1–7 we reported the relative importance ascribed to typical church programs by pastors, seminarians, and laymen. Both pastors and seminarians placed their highest priorities on study groups and social action groups, while the laymen placed greatest importance on church boards and committees and the women's group.

The lowest priorities were placed on men's and women's groups and on church committees by ministers and students, while social action groups, prayer meetings, and retreats were considered to be least important by the laity.

These distinctions suggest that ministers (and seminarians who will be following them into the parish) prefer cognitive and action-oriented church programs. There is also a latent clericalism involved, in the sense that the programs they consider to be most important are those in which the minister generally exercises primary leadership. That both the ministers and students placed the laymen's groups at the bottom of their lists further supports this interpretation.

The laymen, by contrast, place their highest priority precisely where they exercise a significant degree of control in the governance of the church and in its programming, for they esteem most their participation on church boards and committees and in the women's groups.

In Table 1–8 we reported the different ways in which laymen, ministers, and students perceived the work of the minister. Ministers reported that they spent most of their time in "study and sermon preparation," in "office and administrative work," and in "visiting the sick and bereaved." They felt that they spent too much time as administrators and organizers and too little time "working for social justice" and in "sermon preparation." Again, their predisposition toward cognitive and action-oriented ministries is reflected here. These views were shared by the seminary students, who felt that ministers need to spend more time than they now do on social action, teaching, and study.

On the other hand, laymen see their minster spending most of his time in his traditional roles as priest, preacher, and pastor, for they placed at the top of their list his activities as a leader of worship, in sermon preparation, and in visiting the sick and the bereaved. If the minister is criticized, it was usually because he failed to spend enough time looking after his congregation, calling on members and nonmembers, and working with children and young people.

Here, then, is the real gap between pulpit and pew: ministers place their highest values on their roles as preacher and prophet; laymen esteem the ministers' priestly and pastoral roles above all others.

In Chapter 1 we described the nuclear family bias of the residentially based parish church. Laymen join churches primarily for deeply personal and family-centered reasons. Ministers, by contrast, feel that the church ought to be more concerned with the public sector, with social ethics rather than with personal morality. The situation is exacerbated by the pattern of residential segregation that prevails in our society, resulting in local churches which are too often organizations defined by racial, ethnic, or social class interests.

There is a certain ambivalence about the minister's calling. We found that he is well trained to engage in the style of ministry most desired by his parishioners, and when asked what further training he would like to have, he was most likely to select those fields which would further strengthen his role as pastor and preacher. While he expresses a need to be more active in working for social justice, he is least likely to want to pursue further study to become more professional in this role.

To sum up, the fundamental gap between pulpit and pew is found in the ways pastor and people conceive the purpose of the church and its ministry. Ministers and seminary students are committed to a style of ministry that is clergy-dominated and cognitive and action-oriented. The laity, by contrast, are primarily interested in forms of church governance and leadership over which they exercise meaningful control, and in affective ministries of the church which will serve their personal and family needs. All other issues that may divide the minster and his congregation are derived from this basic gap between pulpit and pew.

6

Denominationalism in a United Church

In 1959, shortly after the formation of the United Church of Christ, Charles Y. Glock made the following observation about the new denomination in a monograph addressed to sociologists, assessing the problems and prospects of the sociology of religion in the United States:

> The recent merger of the Congregational Christian and the Evangelical and Reformed Churches is an extreme example of the general trend [toward ecumenicity]. Even given the changing climate of opinion, a merger of these two denominations at this point in history would have seemed highly unlikely. The first denomination has its roots in England, the other in Germany. The first is geographically centered in New England, the other is strongest in Pennsylvania. The two denominations differ sharply in polity and in theology. The Congregational is one of the wealthiest churches in the United States in terms of the per capita income of its members. In contrast, the membership of the Evangelical and Reformed Church is modally lower middle class. Yet a merger has been consummated. It would seem that this kind of event, so different from what our theoretical notions might have led us to expect, should arouse the curiosity of sociologists of religion.[1]

The "theoretical notions" to which Professor Glock refers are, of course, those of H. Richard Niebuhr and his classic study, *The Social Sources of Denominationalism,* which has informed numerous empirical studies of religion in the United States since its publication in 1929.[2] Niebuhr identified socio-economic status, nationalism, sectionalism, immigration, and race as social factors which predispose denominational proliferation in the United States, and from this theoretical perspective the union of the Evangelical and Reformed Church and the Congregational Christian Churches to form the United Church of Christ in 1957 appeared to be a sociological anomaly.

If the United Church of Christ does not represent a sociological anomaly, as Glock's comments seem to suggest, a substantial revision of Niebuhr's "social sources" theory may be required. On the other hand, if the theory is still valid, we should anticipate significant dysfunctions or discontinuities within the new denomination.

It is the hypothesis of this chapter that the social sources theory of denominationalism continues to be valid despite the apparent contradiction suggested by the United Church of Christ, and that the formal "unity" manifested by the union obscures the "denominationalism" which is latent within the religious group.

What is particularly significant about the data at our disposal to test this hypothesis is that it was collected ten years after the union of the two denominations. During this period, most of the national boards and agencies of the uniting groups were merged, but not without making important accommodations to each other. Before turning to our empirical data, it is necessary to describe briefly some of the differences, both sociological and religious, which the two groups brought into the union.

Contrasting Traditions and Practices

Historically, the Congregational Christian churches trace their origins to the English Reformation of the sixteenth century and the Separatists who exiled themselves to Holland under the leadership of Robert Browne to escape the harassment of the established Anglican Church. These Englishmen, growing restive under the Dutch language and the influence of Dutch culture on their children, began looking toward America, and a group of them sailed from Plymouth, England, on the Mayflower in 1620. They were joined by other Separatists and Puritans in due time, and because of their early beginnings their clergy and congregations became very influential in determining the political and social organization of New England.

In the New England colonies, and especially in Massachusetts Bay Colony, Congregational clergymen exercised tremendous power. No one could vote unless he were a church member, and church membership depended on the endorsement of the minister. Congregationalism was the established church of many New England colonies; disestablishment did not come to New Hampshire until 1817 and to Connecticut until a year later. Congregationalism was not disestablished in Massachusetts until 1833.

This hegemony meant that "the Congregational Way" became identified with "the New England Way," with important consequences for shaping the values and institutions of the new nation. Traditional American historians have argued that "the finest flowers of our society had been nurtured in New England," transmitting their culture and institutions to the expanding frontier. One indicator of this is shown in the location of Congregational churches and colleges established outside of New England during the nineteenth century. They are found in greatest numbers in Ohio, Michigan, Illinois, Wisconsin, Minnesota, Iowa, Nebraska, and the Dakotas.[3]

Congregationalism had little interest in establishing itself in the South during the nineteenth century, undoubtedly in part because of the church's abolitionist views. (It should be noted, however, that New England was very deeply involved in the slave trade until it was legally abolished in 1807. Much of New England's seaport economy was dependent on the building and provisioning of slave ships.) After the Civil War, Congregationalists became very active in the establishment of schools for freedmen in the former slave states, and through such special agencies as the American Missionary Association they established and staffed hundreds of schools and a number of colleges for Negroes.[4]

In 1929 the Congregationalists united with the Christian Church, a denomination formed out of three disparate movements in North Carolina, Kentucky, and Vermont. This union was preceded four years earlier by the union of the Congregational Church with the Evangelical Protestant Churches, composed mostly of Germans and German Swiss, which provided an historic precedent for the union that was to take place some three decades later to form the United Church of Christ.

The Evangelical and Reformed Church was formed in 1934 by a union of the Reformed Church in the United States with the Evangelical Synod of North America. The historic roots of this denomination are somewhat more complex to trace, for these groups, though sharing a common background in German and Swiss pietism, emigrated to America about a century apart.

The foundations of the Reformed Church in the United States were laid by early German immigrants from the Palatinate region of Germany in the colonial period of American history. Harassed by long years of controversy between the Lutherans and the Reformed, war, taxation, and economic depression, these immigrants responded to William Penn's promises of brotherhood and prosperity in the New World. From New York and Philadelphia where they landed, they settled over a wide territory, northward up the Hudson River into the Mohawk and Schorharie Valleys, northwestward from Germantown toward Reading, westward into Lancaster and York counties in Pennsylvania, and southward into Maryland and across the Potomac into the Shenandoah valley.

The largest group settled in Pennsylvania and in due time established a college and theological school in Lancaster. During the early period the Reformed churches enjoyed close relations with both the Dutch Reformed Church and the Lutherans, but as their numbers grew they became independent and developed their own institutions. Of particular concern, which they shared with other immigrant groups of the period, was the need to preserve the German language and cultural tradition, and this was done by the establishment of a publishing house and a number of educational institutions.

The Evangelical Synod of North America originated in the same tradition of German Pietism and the Swiss Reformation, but not until a century later. The Prussian King Frederick's attempt early in the nineteenth century to coerce the unification of rival Lutheran and Reformed groups, followed by a series of social and economic deprivations, made conditions ripe for migration to the New World. While most European immigrants during this century entered the United States through the eastern port cities, others came by way of New Orleans and went up the Mississippi River, settling in Missouri and Illinois with St. Louis as their base.

German Evangelical ministers were active in establishing churches throughout this region, and in 1849 they organized a new theological school at Marthasville, Missouri. This school later became Eden Theological Seminary when it was moved to St. Louis. In 1925 it was relocated in Webster Groves, a suburb, where it stands today.

An important social consequence of the Evangelical Synod's pietistic heritage was its major concern for the establishment of benevolent institutions in America. The Synod was especially active in establishing and supporting hospitals and homes for orphans, the aged, and invalids.

According to one chronicler of the union between the Reformed and Evangelical churches, some tensions developed during the "reconstruction period."

> There was a rising fear of ecclesiastical hierarchy. The Reformed pastors were concerned lest their freedom might not be reconcilable with the centralization of the Evangelical Synod. Conciliation was necessary also along liturgical lines. While never a serious subject of controversy, it was apparent that in some areas there was a strong trend toward formalism in the worship services while in others there was a wide latitude of freedom.[5]

During the 23 years of its existence, the Evangelical and Reformed Church divided its administrative responsibilities between two centers of power, Philadelphia and St. Louis, with two publishing houses and seminaries identified with its historic past. Ministers identified with the "E" side of the Church usually attended Elmhurst College and Eden Seminary, while "R" ministers were more likely to have gone to Franklin and Marshall, Catawba, or Ursinus College and then to Lancaster Seminary.

In addition to these historic and cultural differences, there were differences in the relative sizes of the two denominations at the time of the union. In 1957 there were 5,506 local congregations of the Congregational Christian Churches organized into 35 state or regional conferences and conventions. The 2,742 local churches of the Evangelical and Reformed Church were grouped into 33 synods. The church memberships reported by the two denominations were 1,401,407 by the Congregational Christian Churches, and 807,280 by the Evangelical and Reformed Church.

Geographically, the greatest differences in strength between the two denominations were found in the New England states, Pennsylvania, Michigan, and Missouri. In New England, for example, there were 1,564 Congregational churches, accounting for more than 28 per cent of all churches in the denomination. By contrast, there were only eight Evangelical and Reformed congregations located in the New England region.

In Pennsylvania, however, there were 887 Evangelical and Reformed churches, compared with 103 congregations affiliated with the Congregational Christian denomination. In Missouri there were four Evangelical and Reformed churches for every Congregational church. Michigan reported 70 Evangelical and Reformed churches, while the Congregationalists had 224.[6]

Table 6–1 Church-Related Institutions of the United Church of Christ (number of institutions by type and denomination).

Type of Institution	Evangelical & Reformed	Congregational Christian
Educational	12	39
Benevolent:		
Hospitals	10	4
City missions/centers	3	12
Homes for children	10	1
Homes for invalids	2	0
Homes for the aged	17	2

Another significant difference between the two denominations is seen in the statistics of church-related institutions summarized in Table 6–1. If a distinction is to be made, clearly the Evangelical and Reformed Church has placed its major emphasis on "benevolent" institutions, while Congregationalists have emphasized "educational" institutions.[7]

The differences in approach to health, welfare, and education are rooted in the two historic religious traditions described earlier. The New England Congregationalists, being firmly secured in the seat of public power, early opted to care for the homeless and needy through the establishment of publicly supported institutions, since they exercised effective control over the public sector. As a result, rather than establishing orphanages and hospitals under denominational auspices, the early Congregationalists put their effort into the establishment of educational institutions, particularly colleges, which were yet to receive widespread public support. Most of these institutions became public or privately supported and independent of denominational control and subsidy.

In the Evangelical and Reformed tradition, denominationally sponsored health and welfare institutions received wide support for a number of reasons. In the first place, the establishment of such facilities under the auspices of the Church was an important part of the tradition of German pietism, and it was this tradition which the early immigrants transplanted in the New World. Furthermore, as they were a later immigrant group, speaking a different language and not sharing the dominant cultural tradition, caring for their own needy in a compatible cultural setting was deemed inescapable. It is no accident, for example, that church-sponsored agencies have been particularly prominent among the Lutherans as well as among Roman Catholics and Jews in the United States, while such agencies have been singularly de-emphasized by denominations related to the earliest English-speaking colonial settlers in America. Lacking political power and in the face of health and welfare institutions thoroughly in control of the Anglo-Saxon Protestant majority, the manifest function of ethnic institutions in America was to enable minority groups to preserve their distinctive cultural values and practices. The latent function of these institutions was to facilitate a gradual accommodation to the majority culture.

The United Church of Christ, then, is a uniquely American denomination enriched by a diversity of historical antecedents. Drawing its theological resources from the reformation in England, Germany, and Switzerland, its founders in the New World from New England Calvinists and Pennsylvania Dutch pietists, and its social role from the established church and the immigrant church, this denomination is well described as a *uniting* as much as a *united* church. In the light of such diversity, it would be strange indeed if differences in style of ministry and conceptions of the church's mission did not exist. We now turn to some of these differences.

Social Origins of Denominationalism

American churchmen are generally reluctant to discuss the impingement of social class on religious groups, but where religious groups exist as voluntary associations, as they do in the United States, the consequences of "nontheological factors" are both real and significant for the churches. We have already referred to H. Richard Niebuhr's classic essay, *The Social Sources of Denominationalism,* which has provided the basis of numerous social studies of religion in America over four decades.[8]

In studies of social stratification and religion, Congregationalists have usually been placed high among American denominations with Episcopalians and Presbyterians. Reformed and Lutheran bodies in these studies occupy intermediate positions above the Baptists, Roman Catholics, and Protestant sect groups.[9]

If, as Niebuhr argued, social differentiation leads to denominational fragmentation, the weakening of these differentiating factors (that is, language, national origins, economic position, and so forth) ought to lead to church unity. The unification of American Lutheran bodies in recent years, separated in the past for reasons of language and national origin, demonstrates the logic of this hypothesis.[10]

It is our intention to determine whether social distinctions continue to exist between the two denominations which formed the United Church of Christ, and if so, what the consequences may be for the manner in which clergymen are recruited, trained, and carry on their work. If there is a lack of consensus about the purpose of the church and its ministry, it may result in part from the persistence of denominationalism in the United Church of Christ.

Much of the empirical data needed to test our hypothesis have already been presented in previous chapters. In most of our tables, responses were differentiated according to the type of seminary attended. Before returning to some of this data in this new context, we need to look once again at the social class data and the consequences of denominational background for the choice of one's seminary.

Among the 1,191 pastors in our survey, 347 identified their denominational origin in the Evangelical and Reformed Church (E & R) and 330 in the Congregational Christian Churches (C C). Among the seminarians who responded, 134 were raised in the Evangelical and Reformed Church and 203 in Congregational Christian churches. Using one's denominational origin as an independent variable, we look first in Table 6–2 at the type of community in which the person was raised, and then in Table 6–3 at the occupation of the respondent's father.

In these tables we have collapsed the categories and combined the data for ministers and students in order to conserve space. The data confirm what we have already described in Chapter 2 in connection with the socio-economic backgrounds of those attending the several types of theological schools affiliated with the denomination. Here, looking only at the two denominational backgrounds, we find that there is little distinction to be made between pastors and seminarians as far as their rural-urban origins are concerned, but when the data is examined by denominational background, half of those with E & R origins were raised in small towns and rural places, in contrast with 35 per cent of those report-

Table 6–2 Rural-Urban Origins of Respondents
(per cent responding by denominational background).

Type of Community in Which Respondent Grew Up	Pastors			Seminarians		
	Total	E & R	C C	Total	E & R	C C
Number reporting	677	347	330	337	134	203
Rural-small town	43	50	36	40	49	35
Town-small city	26	20	33	32	20	39
Large city-suburb	31	30	31	28	31	26

Table 6–3 Occupation of Respondents' Fathers
(per cent responding by denominational background).

	Pastors			Seminarians		
Father's Occupation	Total	E & R	C C	Total	E & R	C C
Number reporting	677	347	330	337	134	203
White collar worker	54	43	65	57	47	64
Blue collar worker	33	42	25	33	39	29
Farmer	13	15	10	10	14	7

ing C C backgrounds. The largest percentage spread between the two groups occurs in the proportions raised in towns and smaller cities, a type of community in which Congregationalists were more likely to have lived than the others.

For Americans, occupation is a primary indicator of social status. In Table 6–3 we find the distribution of the respondents' fathers' occupations by denominational background. While a significant difference continues to exist between the two groups in terms of the proportions classified in white collar occupations, a comparison between ministers and students raised in the Evangelical and Reformed Church reflects the upward social mobility of that group, in that a higher proportion of the fathers of seminarians are white collar workers and a lower proportion are blue collar workers than the fathers of pastors in the same denomination. This table reflects what is generally occurring in American society as a whole: the decreasing role of agricultural employment and the increasing proportions of the labor force employed in clerical, technical, and professional work.

What these tables suggest about the relative social status of the two denominational groups is confirmed by responses to the question, "How would you compare the prestige or social status of your father's usual occupation with that of the Protestant minister today?" Five per cent of the pastors and 8 per cent of the seminarians with E & R backgrounds reported that their fathers' status was higher than that of the minister. By contrast, 14 per cent of the C C pastors and 20 per cent of the C C students placed the occupation of their fathers above that of the Protestant minister in prestige and social status.

In short, both in terms of the indicators we have used and in terms of the respondents' subjective evaluation of social status as it is generally conceived in American society, social class differences continue to exist between the two denominational groups which make up the United Church of Christ.

We turn next to a description of the effect that denominational background has on the type of seminary the individual selects to pursue his education for the ministry.

Denomination and Choice of School

On the basis of what we have described earlier about the development of parallel health, education, and welfare institutions by later immigrant groups in America, we would anticipate that there would be a greater tendency for respondents coming from the Evangelical and Reformed tradition to seek their education in denominational institutions, while former Congregationalists would be more likely to have attended nondenominational or public colleges and interdenominational theological schools. These expectations are clearly fulfilled in the data reported in Tables 6–4 and 6–5, in which

Table 6–4 Type of Undergraduate Institution Attended (per cent responding by denominational background).

Type of College/ University	Pastors			Seminarians		
	Total	E & R	C C	Total	E & R	C C
Number reporting	677	347	330	337	134	203
Municipal, city, community	2	3	4	3	0	4
State college or university	14	16	29	26	23	29
Private, nonsectarian	16	7	33	24	6	36
Denominational	20	77	41	48	73	32
Other	*	1	0	1	1	1

* Less than 0.5 per cent.

Table 6–5 Type of Theological Seminary Attended (per cent responding by denominational background).

Type of Seminary	Pastors			Seminarians		
	Total	E & R	C C	Total	E & R	C C
Number reporting	677	347	330	337	134	203
Evangelical and Reformed	44	80	6	35	77	8
Congregational Christian	21	3	40	35	9	52
Interdenominational	21	7	36	30	14	40
Other Denomination	14	10	18			

denominational backgrounds are related to the type of college and seminary attended.

Among the pastors, we note first that 77 per cent of the E & R's and 41 per cent of the C C's attended denominationally related colleges as undergraduates. Furthermore, Congregational-background pastors were more than four times as likely as others to have attended private, nonsectarian colleges and universities, and nearly twice as likely to have attended a public university than their E & R cohorts.

Among the seminary students, while a higher proportion with backgrounds in the Evangelical and Reformed Church attended a state college or university, 73 per cent of them did their undergraduate work in a denominational school. Congregational-background seminarians were distributed almost equally among state, private, and denominational institutions.

This predisposition to favor denominational educational institutions is even greater when one examines the choice of seminary. According to Table 6–5, 80 per cent of the E & R ministers and 40 per cent of the C C ministers attended seminaries related to their respective denominations. More than half of the C C clergymen received their theological education in interdenominational seminaries or in schools related to other denominations. By contrast, only 17 per cent of the E & R ministers attended interdenominational seminaries or those of other denominations.

Although the data is not included, it should be mentioned that the majority of the 514 pastors in our survey who were originally members of other denominations received their theological education in one of the thirteen seminaries affiliated with the United Church of Christ. Twelve per cent of these pastors attended former Evangelical and Reformed seminaries, 23 per cent attended former Congregational Christian schools, and 26 per cent received their professional training in one of the seven ecumenical schools related to the denomination. The remaining 39 per cent of this group were educated in seminaries of other denominations.

The pattern of seminary selection on the part of students is similar to that of pastors. Three out of four seminarians with origins in the Evangelical and Reformed Church attended denominational colleges and denominational seminaries. Congregational-background students, like the pastors, are distributed among state, private, and denominational undergraduate schools and between denominational and interdenominational seminaries for their professional education.

Using the choice of college and seminary as an indicator, then, we conclude from these tables that denominationalism is more salient for respondents rooted in the Evangelical and Reformed Church than it is for those whose origins were in the Congregational Christian Churches.

Denominationalism and Styles of Ministry

We are now in a position to return to the data reported in previous chapters. We noted in table after table as we described the characteristics of the education of our respondents and their conceptions of the minister's work that the type of seminary with which the respondent was identified was a significant independent variable. In describing their perceptions, attitudes, and activities, those who were related to former Evangelical and Reformed seminaries tended to fall at one end of a continuum, while respondents from interdenominational schools occupied the opposite end, with Congregational Christian respondents usually occupying an intervening position.

In one sense, the continuum could be characterized as moving from conservatism to liberalism, or from the support of traditional values and forms to new values and new forms of ministry. Depending on one's perspective, such characterizations can be both pejorative and invidious. What we have, rather, are differentiating styles of ministry that are the consequences of different styles of theological education.

These styles of education and ministry will be elaborated more fully in Chapter 7. Here we shall merely mention them as they relate to the basic theme of this chapter—that denominational background has significant consequences for the way in which ministers are educated and the way in which they perceive their professional role.

Three basic styles of ministry emerge from our findings: the *institutional style,* with its orientation toward the denomination; the *individualistic style,* which is oriented toward the parishioner; and the *social style,* with its orientation toward society.

These distinctive styles of education and ministry are further identified with the three basic groups of seminaries in which clergymen of the United Church of Christ receive their professional training. As a group, graduates and currently enrolled students of the Evangelical and Reformed seminaries are best characterized by the *institutional style,* since they were most likely to be denominationally oriented among our survey groups. The majority of them attended denominationally related colleges and seminaries for their education, were most committed to traditional forms of parish ministry, placed a high value on knowledge about denominational programs and policies, and were least critical of the various aspects of the church's life.

To the extent that the graduates and seminarians related to the interdenominational schools shared views opposite to those we have just described, and to the extent that their attitudes toward controversial social issues were the most liberal of all groups, we would identify this group of respondents with the *social style* of education and ministry.

Respondents related to the Congregational Christian seminaries, in turn, would be characterized by the *individualistic style,* which is oriented toward the parishioner. The principal factor here is our finding that greater emphasis is placed on Religion and Personality as a major field of study on the part of respondents in this group and, in the words of the Harrison Report, "in Religion and Personality the former Congregationalists shine out like an individualistic light. No other group approaches them in their interest in this field."[11]

These characterizations are neither exclusive nor dominant. Needless to say, all the seminaries in one way or another address themselves to all of these styles of ministry. As we have examined our findings, the identifications we have made between seminary type and style of ministry seemed most appropriate to us. No priority of styles is intended or suggested, for all of these dimensions are essential for the education and work of the minister.

7

Toward a Theory of the Ministry

The purpose of this final chapter is to summarize the findings of our research along two dimensions: from a sociological perspective within a theory of the professions, and from the perspective of religion through an elaboration of a theory of the ministry. We began this study of pastors and seminarians with a note of vocational crisis and we return to this theme, for the uncertainty of the minister's calling is also the uncertainty of the Church in today's world.

The Ministry as a Profession

To discuss the ministry as a "profession" implies some doubt or ambiguity about the clergyman's professional status. The concept "profession" is etymologically derived from the adjective "professed," which had reference to vows taken by a religious order. The term was secularized by the seventeenth century to refer to the occupation an individual professed to be skilled in and to follow. The "learned professions" were identified as law, divinity, and medicine.[1]

For example, W. J. Reader's study of professional men in nineteenth-century England begins with a discussion of "Divinity, Physic and Law" as the normative professions of that period.[2] Daniel H. Calhoun's case studies of professional lives in America deal with a medical community in New York, lawyers of the Cumberland River country in Tennessee, and clergymen in New Hampshire.[3] In an historical sense, there is no ambiguity about the ministry as a profession.

The professional status of the ministry is a problem; in fact, the professions as a whole have become problematical. The social and technological changes of this century have changed not only the character of work but of the professions as well. The literature is replete with descriptions of "emerging" and "new" professions, of "semi-professions," and of the professionalization of nonprofessions and the nonprofessional character of traditional professions.

Wilbert E. Moore's recent volume on the roles and rules of the professions devotes more than 50 pages to a "selected" bibliography on the subject. Some of the titles listed are indicative of the present ferment: "The Social Status of Teachers," "The Science Administrator: A New Profession," "The Emerging Profession of Business," and the "Unionization of Professional Engineers and Chemists."[4] In a volume of essays edited by Amitai Etzioni, the concept "semi-profession" is used to describe the work and organization of teachers, nurses, and social workers.[5]

The more dramatic instances of crisis among professionals have occurred at recent annual meetings of professional societies, particularly among academicians in the humanities and social sciences, but frequently among lawyers and medical doctors as well. Since the mid-1960s the scholarly and detached deliberations of scientists, sociologists, modern language scholars, and historians have been marked by noisy and angry disputes over civil rights, women's rights, and the war in Vietnam. When the American Historical Association rejected an anti-war resolution in 1970 as being "out of order" and not pertaining to the purposes and functions of historians as such, a radical caucus returned the following year with a statement that pointed to the central issue: "It is crucially important that people who consider themselves political radicals and who also consider themselves historians should avoid a disjuncture between the two roles."[6]

To reflect on the ministry as a profession, we shall use Talcott Parsons' well-known essay, "The Professions and Social Structure," as the theoretical framework. Parsons was aware that "many of the most important features of our society are to a considerable extent dependent on the smooth functioning of the professions," and that "our most important social functions are carried on" in the institutional framework of the professions.[7] This is a sociological way of saying what we observed at the outset: the problem of the minister's vocation is nothing more than the problem of the church in today's world.

The Service Function

According to Parsons, the first characteristic of the professional man is the assumption that he is not "engaged in the pursuit of his personal profit, but in the performance of services to his patients or clients, or to impersonal values like the advancement of science."[8]

There can be little doubt in anyone's mind that the ministry is not a profit-making occupation but one of providing services. The minister's primary "clients" are his parishioners, particularly when one considers the clergyman's profession in an institutional framework. He is called to be the pastor of a particular congregation at a particular time and place. While he may see himself in more universalistic terms as "the servant of Christ," with the whole world as his "parish," most of the ministers about whom we are concerned in this study have a very special, if not primary, responsibility to serve a specific social group which is his congregation.

The institutional setting in which the minister does his

work is an important aspect of his role definition. In their study of the ministers of Little Rock during the crisis over the admission of Negro students to the Central High School in 1957, Campbell and Pettigrew identified three reference systems which contributed to the moral dilemma of the ministers: the self, the profession, and the congregation. The ministers remained inactive during the racial crisis because the institutional structure, particularly their professional and parishioner reference systems, compelled them to maintain a peaceable atmosphere rather than to give leadership to social reform.[9]

While service to his congregation is primary, the minister as a professional man is also engaged in service to such impersonal values as justice, peace, and morality. His service to these values may be only indirectly related to his service to his parishioners; he may take to the streets and join a picket line, serve on the community's human relations commission, or sign a petition for peace.

This dual possibility for service suggests an explanation for the vocational crisis of the minister described in Chapter 1 and the gap between pulpit and pew which was taken up in Chapter 5. We found, for example, that men who were most firmly committed to serve as pastors of residentially based parish churches were least likely to entertain thoughts of leaving the ministry for some other vocation. On the other hand, we found those who expressed highest concern for serving impersonal values, such as the churches' involvement in social issues, were most likely to think of leaving the ministry and least interested in serving as pastors of local churches.

The minister's primary client—the parishioner—defines the minister's role predominantly in the professional-client relationship, rather than in the professional-impersonal value mode. The service he expects from his pastor is highly individualized in terms of his personal and familial needs. When evaluating the relative importance of church programs, pastors and seminarians place their highest priorities on the more cognitive and impersonal values, such as study groups and social action; laymen, by contrast, place their priorities on their personal involvement in church activities, such as church boards and committees, and in laymen's groups where they exercise control.

In theory the church has accommodated itself to this conflict between service to persons and service to impersonal values by developing nonparochial or paraparochial forms of ministry. The more impersonal forms of ministry have, however, depended on the financial support of residentially based congregations. Thus the present crisis in the church and the uncertainty of the minister's calling is in part a function of its institutional structure. In its present institutionalized form, residentially based parish churches are most functional as instruments of comfort; nonparochial religious organizations, including denominational boards and agencies, are better equipped to serve the challenging function.

Phillip E. Hammond's study of campus ministers is an example of one way in which the church has tried to meet the minister's role conflict by providing an alternative institutional structure. Hammond observes that "campus clergy *are* systematically different from parish clergy," and the campus ministry is one way in which "mavericks" in the profession can remain in the church while removing themselves from its primary institutional context.[10]

To be a professional, then, the minister needs to understand his dual responsibility. By serving exclusively the personal needs of his parishioners, he is often accused and made to feel guilty of being socially irrelevant or trivial in his ministry; by concentrating on his service to impersonal values, he is tempted to neglect the personal needs of his parishioners, which may be very real and urgent. If he alienates them sufficiently he will lose the institutional support he needs to carry on his ministry.

The Basis of Authority

The second important characteristic of the professional man is that he "exercises authority . . . based on superior technical competence."[11] Parsons is not referring here to certain kinds of authority, such as those based on church tradition or the authority of Scripture, which are important to clergymen. The authority of the professional from Parsons' sociological perspective is based on "technical" knowledge and is limited to this narrowly defined technical sphere. He refers to this type of authority as the "specificity of function."

In our research we found that the laymen are quite clear as to what is functionally specific about the ministry. When asked to describe the ways in which they think ministers spend their time, they mention most often leading worship, preaching, and pastoral care. These laymen also feel that ministers spend "too much time" in office administration, as social reformers, and as fund raisers.

The laymen's responses identify the functions that are most specific to the minister, the traditional roles of priest, preacher, and pastor. The roles they criticize are those performed by others in society, for they can be done equally well by businessmen, union leaders, or housewives.

If the laymen seem to be clear about what is functionally specific about the ministry, pastors and theological students reflect some uncertainty and ambivalence. The problem centers primarily around the priority given to the role of "working for social justice" by the clergy and their student cohorts. The prophetic witness of Amos and Jeremiah provides an impressive Biblical basis for the claim that social reform is among the central functions of the church, but in our present discussion it is hardly "functionally specific" to the clergyman's profession. That social justice is a major, if not central, concern of the church is not the issue. The issue is whether or not the minister's role as a professional practitioner is to be defined in terms of the social reform function.

According to our data, the parishioner, the minister's primary client, does not include social reform as an attribute of the minister's role. It is certainly not functionally specific or differentiating as far as the ministry as a profession is concerned. Social reformers can be recruited from all walks of life; they may be clergymen, but not necessarily so. What, then, is the content of the minister's technical competence on which his authority is based? Our research suggests that it is his knowledge of the Bible and Theology.

Ministers claim to know more about the Bible and Theology than the laity; these are the areas of his superior "technical" competence and the basis of his professional authority.

Thus it is no accident that the majority of the pastors and seminarians in this study majored in Bible or Theology as theological students, that courses in these fields were thought to be the most helpful to them in their training, and that church programs such as study groups and preaching were given highest priority.

Furthermore, the minister's pre-theological education and his desire for continuing education provide little support for his social reform impulses in any professional or technical sense. One might assume that a professional social reformer would include among his "superior technical competence" a degree of expertise in such fields as social organization, economics, political science, and other related areas. Less than one respondent in five selected the social sciences as areas for further study which might be helpful to his professional growth and competence.

There are many ministers who have developed a high degree of technical competence as a basis for their authority as social reformers, but the majority possess only a layman's knowledge of social organization and political processes needed for reform. Ministers are probably more "technically" trained as moralists to deal with problems of personal relationships than as social ethicists to deal with the more impersonal problems of social and political change. The former is an area of functional specificity for ministers; the latter, while significant and functional, is not unique to the minister's profession.

Autonomy

The third characteristic which distinguishes a profession is that status in the profession "is to a high degree independent of status in kinship groups, the neighborhood and the like, in short from what are sometimes called primary group relationships."[12] The status of the professional man is judged on the basis of universalistic criteria determined by one's professional peers and is not subject to the particularism of local groups.

A minister may thus be judged "incompetent" and thrown out of his pulpit by a local congregation because he was at odds with the power elite in the congregation or violated the mores of the community. His professional status would not be compromised under such conditions if, in the judgment of his professional peers, he had remained faithful to the established canons of his profession.

Professionals are usually organized into societies, which function to regularize professional status and to oversee the ethical behavior of their members. One of the problems for the ministry as a profession is that the minister is not a member of a professional society in the usual sense of the term. Unlike doctors or lawyers or sociologists, who belong to national professional societies, clergymen are more often related to local judicatory groups that are denominationally fragmented and whose memberships change as the minister moves from one locality to another. Ecumenical ministerial groups are often nothing more than "anti-poaching" societies. This term was used by Vidich and Bensman to characterize the ministers' group of Springdale, a small town in upstate New York. As "professionals" sharing a common calling, they met regularly to plan community-wide religious observances, made arrangements to look after one another's parishioners during their summer vacations, but most importantly made sure that denominational prerogatives were observed when new families moved into town.[13]

If there is a major weakness in the professional character of the ministry, it is perhaps at this point, for too often the minister's achievement and competence is judged by particularistic rather than by universalistic criteria, by local boards and congregations rather than by the profession at large. The experience of the Little Rock ministers cited earlier is a case in point. The criteria used by the professional reference group—the local ministerium—to judge the behavior of the city's ministers were particularistic rather than universal, local rather than national. In fact, many ministers acknowledged that their attitudes and behavior were inconsistent with positions taken by their denominational bodies on the racial situation.[14]

The organization of The Academy of Parish Clergy a few years ago provides some promise for an authentic professional society for clergymen. If the Academy gets preoccupied solely with raising ministers' salaries and upgrading educational requirements, however, it will become a trade union rather than a professional society. Such concerns are not alien to the concerns of professional societies, though they may serve functional needs of the profession.

Functional equivalents for the ministry do exist. They are largely groups of specialized professionals in such areas as pastoral counseling, religious education, religious research, and the various academic fields among theological educators. As other professional societies, these groups are organized nationally, publish journals, hold conventions, read papers for critical peer evaluation, and otherwise maintain their identity. The Academy of Parish Clergy may in time do for the parish pastor what the American Medical Association does for the practicing doctor.

Goals and Achievement

The fourth characteristic of professionalism suggested by Parsons has to do with the problem of self interest and its correlate, the goal of the professional. Put another way, what is it that the professional is trying to achieve, and how is his achievement recognized?

The professional practitioner presumably seeks "success." But success is meaningless without recognition. The medical doctor's success may be objectively measured by the number of people he cures or the number of babies he brings into the world. The "symbols of recognition" may be community respect, the esteem of his professional peers, and the growth of his practice and wealth.

Ministers, too, seek success as professional practitioners. There are those who keep careful records of the number of baptisms, weddings, and funerals conducted, the number of pastoral calls made, or sermons preached. For others, the visible "symbols of recognition" are to be found in the growing statistics of church membership, attendance, and giving which are reported each year to denominational headquarters. Success is also objectified by promotions up the hierarchical ladder, by moving from smaller to larger churches, from lesser to greater responsibilities.

But these indicators of success and achievement are culturally determined and for many irrelevant to the minister's professional goals. Much of what the minister does cannot be defined in terms of objective achievement or be made subject to recognition by one's peers. Often what is most objectively discernible, such as the increase in institutional strength, may not be esteemed by one's peers. At other times, the minister's "success" in leading an unpopular cause may be subject to criticism rather than praise. The conflict between ministries of comfort and ministries of challenge, between ministries to individuals and families and ministries to impersonal social values, between the need for institutional survival and the call to lose one's life in order to find it, all point to tensions which prevail in church and ministry. Such tensions are functional for the profession so long as they provide the context for self-criticism and motivation to explore new ideas and new techniques for the achievement of the more fundamental purposes of the church and its ministry.

Clergymen have an understandable reluctance to speak of their profession in terms of "success" and "achievement," for the minister's calling transcends the content generally given to these terms. What he does want are "support systems" adequate to help him cope with the changing needs of his profession.

The Professions and the University

One further dimension of professionalism needs to be mentioned before concluding this section. It is the role of the university in the training of the professional. Bernard Barber argues that the more professional a profession is, the more likely it is to train its recruits in university-related schools. One of the characteristics of "emerging or marginal professions" is to "locate themselves in universities" when they are trying "to raise standards for themselves."[15]

Barber lists a number of advantages provided by a university-based professional school. One of its basic functions is "the transmission to its students of the generalized and systematic knowledge that is the basis of professional performance." The professional school "can borrow resources of knowledge" from other departments, co-opt teaching and research resources, and in other ways get the cooperation of the university community.[16]

He sees the university professional schools as "the leading, though not the sole, innovators and systematizers of ideas for their professions" and the professional school faculty as "ethical role models" for their students. Perhaps most important for Barber is the detachment of the university professional school from the profession:

> For both its knowledge and its ethical functions, the relative insulation of the university professional school has certain advantages. It is relatively freer of those commitments to other organizations and other interests that practicing professionals have, and therefore it is more nearly able to maintain the highest intellectual and moral standards. Also, it can use the general insulation of the university from certain pressures to fortify itself in the performance of its functions, sometimes even in the face of resistance or opposition from the practicing professionals themselves.[17]

Of the thirteen seminaries related to the United Church of Christ, four are located in major universities: Harvard, Howard, Vanderbilt, and Yale. All of these university-located schools are interdenominational. Two of the three remaining interdenominational seminaries, Pacific and Union, though not in universities, are located adjacent to them, so that the functions mentioned by Barber can be served in the training of ministers.

Only Chicago Theological Seminary, among the six denominational institutions, is located on the campus of a major university and enjoys the advantages of a university relationship.

University-based professional education is not perceived to be important by the majority of our respondents, including those who have been educated in such schools. In our study, only 29 per cent of the pastors and 37 per cent of the seminarians attached great importance to university-related theological education. Support for this notion ranged from only 16 per cent of both pastors and students of Evangelical and Reformed seminaries to a little over 40 per cent of the interdenominational school respondents.

Our survey has shown that respondents attending university-related schools are indeed freer of institutional commitments, tend to be more critical of the profession and its institutional framework, and are more open to alternative styles of work and education. University-based professional education is dysfunctional for the denomination in the sense that the church exercises little or no control over the student's technical training and has little opportunity to elicit the student's loyalty or commitment to the organization.

The relatively low priority placed on theological education in a university context may in part result from the present crisis in the university itself. Pastors and seminarians may be as uncertain about the purposes and functions of the university as they are about the church today.

The Profession in Retrospect

In the light of all this, the professional status of the ministry is clearly a problem. The minister is a professional man in the sense that he is engaged in service to his parishioners and to the community at large. His professional authority is unquestionably based on his superior technical competence—principally his expert knowledge of Bible and Theology—and he applies this knowledge in the performance of functionally specific roles as preacher, priest, and pastor.

The ministry is less than professional in the sense that clergymen are not organized into professional societies which function to guard the esoteric knowledge and skills of the profession, set up standards of recruitment and performance, pursue new knowledge, meet regularly, and publish journals.

Organizations of ministers are fragmented by denominationalism, are usually local in scope, and their memberships are transitory because of the minister's geographic mobility.

It is the denomination rather than the profession which legitimates the minister's occupational status. Particularly if he attends a denominational seminary, his training, work, and continuing education tend to be less than universalistic, for such seminaries are often isolated institutions without convenient access to the "generalized and systematic knowledge" which would be found in the university.

One major source of the contemporary minister's uncertainty about his calling is that his role as a leader of social reform is not functionally specific to his profession. While he may speak with authority about the normative aspects of social problems to the extent that his authority is derived from his superior technical knowledge of Bible and Theology, he lacks superior technical competence in areas most crucial to the solution of complex social and economic problems of modern society. Thus when he speaks out on these issues, he does so more as a well-informed layman than as a technical expert, as a civic-minded citizen rather than as a professional practitioner.

It is therefore no accident that some clergymen leave parochial ministries when they have developed technical competence as social reformers, for the parish church is often dysfunctional for their professional goals. Some of these men find positions within the church in nonparochial ministries, such as in specialized work in disadvantaged communities or as campus ministers. The study of "ex-pastors" by Jud and his colleagues reported that "social service or social change" was mentioned by nearly one-third of their respondents as the area of current employment. One ex-pastor in five found himself in secular education, and nearly the same proportion in other professions.[18] In such settings, the professional minister's new "clients" are more likely to perceive the functional specificity of his new role, and he is also likely to be more satisfied in his new setting because the needed "symbols of recognition" are less ambiguously at his disposal.

Styles of Education and Ministry

At the conclusion of Chapter 6 we described tentatively three basic styles of ministry that have emerged from our research. While elements of each style are to be found in all seminaries related to the United Church of Christ, we identified each style with one of the three major groups of seminaries we have studied.

The styles of education and ministry we shall elaborate now are "ideal types" in sociological terms. As theoretical constructions, ideal types are *typical* patterns of meaning which have been abstracted from our data. The types are "ideal" in the conceptual and not the normative sense, and since they are abstractions they do not exist in reality as pure types. They provide us with a heuristic method to develop a theory of education and ministry.[19]

The *institutional style* of education and ministry is characterized by a strong commitment to one's denomination. This commitment is nurtured in childhood by the active participation of the future minister's family in a local church. The pastor of the individual's local church is the "significant other" or primary role model who is most helpful in arriving at the decision to enter the Christian ministry.

His decision to attend a denominationally related college and the seminary of his denomination is encouraged by the peer group to which he belongs. To the extent that ethnicity continues to be a source of denominationalism in American Protestantism, denominational loyalty is esteemed as a means of preserving the distinctive cultural values of the ethnic group.

This sense of denominational loyalty means there is a corresponding commitment to serve the parish church. In contrast with other styles of ministry, the institutionally oriented minister is less critical of traditional forms of church organization and is least likely to entertain thoughts of leaving the ministry for some other vocation.

His commitment to the parish church is reflected in the kinds of courses he took in seminary and those he considered to be most helpful in preparing him for his work. He was likely to have majored in Bible or Theology, subjects most unique to his profession, but he places a higher priority than others on Practical Theology as an alternative area of concentration. His field work experience while a seminarian was most likely to have been in a local church and is positively evaluated. For his continuing education, the institutionally oriented minister would like most to gain more competence in the practical fields, such as preaching and Christian education.

He minimizes the importance of a university-related theological education and the necessity for the minister to develop expertise in nonreligious areas of knowledge. He considers his knowledge of the denomination's program and structure to be relatively more important than others.

As a consequence of the social group to which he belongs and the relative homogeneity of his college and seminary experience, his attitudes toward controversial social issues are more conservative than those who are oriented toward other styles of ministry.

The institutional style of education and ministry is most functional for the growth and preservation of the denomination's identity and its prevailing institutional structure.

The *individualistic style* of ministry is primarily concerned with the pastor's relationship to his parishioners. In the training of the minister, a serious and systematic attempt is made to provide him with technical competence in a nonreligious field (Psychology) in addition to the traditional fields of Bible and Theology. Like the institutional style of education, well-supervised field work in the parish and knowledge of the practical field are given high priority during the minister's theological education.

His undergraduate studies take place almost equally in public, private, and denominational colleges, and though he is most likely to have majored in the humanities, the individualistically oriented minister was more likely than others to have majored in the social sciences.

On controversial social issues, while generally liberal, this type of minister is in the middle of the road when it comes to the institutional form of the church. Politically, the majority in this group identify themselves with the Democrats, but if they are Republicans, they are most likely to be found among the individualistically oriented ministers.

As a group, these ministers are more likely than others to have majored in Religion and Personality while in seminary: this derives in part from the emphases of the seminaries themselves in providing more resources for study in this area, and in part from the seminarian having a greater personal need for such courses.

In many ways, and particularly in evaluating traditional forms of the church and its ministry, parishioner oriented ministers lean more in the direction of the socially oriented rather than the institutionally oriented style of education and ministry. Their criticism of the existing form of the parish church, of theological education, and of society, as well as their thoughts of leaving the ministry for another vocation, is strong, though not as strong as it is for the socially oriented minister.

The parishioner-oriented minister continues to maintain a high degree of support for his denomination and its institutions in spite of his critical outlook, and in this sense this style of ministry is also functional for the denomination.

For the *social style* of education and ministry, society, rather than the denomination or parishioner, is the primary orientation that defines the purpose of the church and its ministry. Its dominant characteristics are to be distinguished most from the institutional style of ministry.

Relative to the other two types, socially oriented ministers are recruited from higher status social groups and from a wider range of denominational backgrounds and educational institutions.

While the individual's pastor is most frequently mentioned as being very helpful in his decision to enter the ministry, the role of the campus pastor is also important for this group.

The social style of ministry is most critical of established institutional forms of the church and most uncertain about remaining in the profession. As seminarians, the majority are not interested in the pastoral ministry; their commitment to denominationalism is low.

These ministers take the most liberal positions on controversial social issues. In their theological education, next to Bible and Theology they are most likely to major in Ethics and Society. While in seminary, "national politics" was the most controversial student issue.

Since they are trained in interdenominational seminaries related to major universities, they place higher value on university-related theological education than those who attend denominational schools. They also consider the development of expertise in a nonreligious field of knowledge to be very important for the minister's education, as well as being made knowledgeable about social movements and techniques of political action. They are most active among the three types on social issues.

Such fields of study in seminary as the practical field, knowledge about denominational programs and structures, and supervised field intern programs in the parish are low priorities for the social style of ministry.

Among students attending seminaries reflecting this style of education, a larger proportion would rather be college or seminary teachers than parish ministers. Like other students, however, they do not possess the "technical competence" to fill such positions.

The social style of education and ministry is in one sense least functional for maintaining the traditional forms of the church and its ministry, but in another sense most promising for the emergence of new forms of theological education and ministry. The heterogeneity of the educational environment and the fluidity of vocational commitment are made possible in the interdenominational seminaries by the absence of direct denominational controls and expectations.

These, then, are the dominant styles of education and ministry which prevail in the United Church of Christ: the *institutional style,* which is oriented toward the denomination; the *individualistic style,* with its orientation toward the parishioner; and the *social style,* which focuses primarily on the larger community. As ideal types, the descriptions we have given are theoretical constructions that have been abstracted from our research to enable us to describe with greater precision the ways in which ministers are educated in the United Church of Christ.

Denominationalism versus Pluralism

In viewing this study in retrospect, the United Church of Christ is characterized as an extremely heterogeneous denomination. Historically rooted in the traditions of English Separatism and German Pietism, the two denominations brought a rich variety of gifts and practices into their union. This survey was conducted a decade after the United Church of Christ was formed; we have found among its clergy and seminary students a pluralism of theological beliefs, of styles of education and ministry.

We use the term "pluralism" rather than "denominationalism" because the distinctions we have noted are more than dichotomous. Theologically, for example, our respondents identified themselves along every theological position from liberal-theism to Biblical conservatism, with the modal group spreading themselves over four variants of neo-orthodoxy.

We have described three distinctive styles of education and ministry, significant differences in attitude toward controversial social issues, a multiplicity of political preferences, and different degrees of commitment to denominational traditions and institutions.

If a strong sense of denominationalism persists in the United Church of Christ, we find it expressed most clearly in the fact that those who were raised in the Evangelical and Reformed tradition continue in major part to attend denominational colleges and to pursue their theological training in former Evangelical and Reformed seminaries.

The type of seminary one attends is a significant intervening variable between one's denominational or social origins and the style of ministry he chooses. The pluralism of beliefs, attitudes, and practices that exists is a function of the wide choice available among the seminaries that train ministers for the denomination. A consequence of such diversity may mean a confusion for the denomination about the purpose of the church and its ministry; it could mean an unparalleled opportunity for the denomination to address its ministry to the world, freed from traditional methods and expectations, with bold imagination and openness.

One of the temptations we face is a tendency to polarize our options when faced by a choice of competing values. When we describe the purpose of the church and its ministry in terms of the "comfort-challenge" dichotomy, the choice is too often framed in terms of "either/or" or in invidious ways. This dilemma was highlighted in our discussion about the role of the minister as a social reformer.

To argue as we did that this role is not functionally specific to the minister's profession may be interpreted by some to mean that we are suggesting the minister should give up his social activist stance and concentrate on what is functionally most specific to his profession: preach, lead worship, and visit the sick. Our data convince us that these are the roles for which he is primarily trained and which he is able to perform well. He does now, and is likely to continue to place high priority on his traditional roles. However, to abdicate his role as a social reformer is to abdicate what is also essential to his ministry.

The minister's inability to perform his prophetic role with any degree of adequacy comparable to his traditional roles is based, we believe, on the structural inadequacy of the church as a social organization. Local congregations served by the overwhelming number of our ministers are usually residentially based, nuclear-family oriented, separated by social class, ethnically and racially segregated, and in most cases based on primary group relationships.

The social issues which concern ministers—institutionalized racism, war, poverty, welfare reform, women's rights, and so forth—are primarily in the realm of secondary relationships, and their solutions must be found for the most part in the political realm.

Ministers do, in their preaching and pastoral care, educate and morally sensitize their parishioners about these social issues, but when they try to organize their congregations to act politically on specific issues, they are often unsuccessful. They fail because the primary organizational goal of the typical residentially based congregation is not social reform.

The experience of Harold R. Fray, Jr., pastor of The Eliot Church of Newton, Massachusetts, is instructive. He has written a moving account of what happened to him and his parishioners when they decided to make a public witness for peace following America's invasion of Cambodia and the tragic events which followed at Kent State and Jackson State universities in the spring of 1970.[20]

The action began when some 50 members of the congregation held a demonstration on the front lawn of the church. This "created a crisis both within the church and community." For 12 hours each day, members of The Eliot Church "were joined by scores of others in the community who welcomed an opportunity to give witness to their outrage and indignation."

According to Fray, this activity gave to those who participated a new sense of community, and because their minister kept central the Biblical and theological bases of their witness throughout many difficult weeks, they also found new meaning in the Christian faith.

But for others in the congregation and community, the occasion brought anger, frustration, and alienation. Some long-term members of the congregation withdrew their financial support; others withdrew from the church altogether. The pastor's comments at the end of his vivid report speak to the problematic nature of the purpose of the church and its ministry today:

> At this crossroad of wide differences, suspicion and mistrust lies the pain of a Christian community seeking to respond to the moral dilemmas of our time, and discovering an internal brokenness and alienation that seem insurmountable at the moment. Understandably one could ask: is it worth it? To what does Jesus call us today?[21]

A more general observation speaks most directly to our concern about the education of today's minister:

> . . . the minister of the local church today discovers that he is not trained sufficiently for the tasks thrust upon him through the vision that he does possess. His theological, Biblical, historical training may be excellent. Yet, he discovers that this does not equip him to cope with the crunch when he seeks to put his leadership into practice.[22]

He goes on to say that "it is this prophetic side of Christian ministry, responsive to social ills and collective human needs, that is the neglected work of the local church today."[23]

The church has met this need for action-oriented ministries in the past by organizing nonparochial and paraparochial forms of the church. These have ranged from denominational home-mission boards, which pass resolutions on controversial social issues and thereby establish norms for church action, to specialized agencies to deal with social issues. In recent years a number of such agencies have been organized, such as the Joint Strategy and Action Committee, Inc., The Interreligious Foundation for Community Organization, and the United Ministries in Higher Education. Most recently a Task Force on Women in Church and Society has been formed to act in the movement for women's rights. Many of these ministries are ecumenical and all are supported by the contributions of local churches through their giving to the denomination.

But what of the prophetic witness of the local church? We are faced with the unsettling fact that one-fifth of the pastors and one-third of the seminarians in this survey still find "a strong appeal" in the notion of leaving the ministry for some other vocation. How can the church conserve the leadership of these men, in whose nurture and training much has been invested?

We stand with the critics of the church who say that the church must become more relevant to the major social issues of our day. We agree with them that alternative institutional structures for the church must be established so that the residentially based parish church does not continue to be the only viable form of ministry for the seminary graduate.

However, we do not agree when critics of the residentially based parish church also argue that the "traditional" churches are irrelevant because they are, for the most part, preoccupied with the privatized sector or with the comforting role. One infers from such criticisms that ministries of comfort to individuals and families are somehow inferior to ministries to social values.

We find the counsel "Come unto me, all ye that labor and are heavy laden, and I will give you rest" to be as Biblically compelling as the injunction to "Let justice roll down as waters, and righteousness as a mighty stream!" The church is called to comfort and to challenge with equal faithfulness.

It may be that the denigration of the comforting role of the church is a rhetorical device necessary to awaken the church from its apathy so it can respond to the social concerns of our times. However, there is a profound relevance about the church's ministry to the privatized sector in times of social stress. In his Lyman Beecher Lectures in 1963, Browne Barr suggested that the minister might be handed a special text to remind him of his responsibility. The text he thought most appropriate was from Galatians 6:10: "Do good to all men . . . especially to those who are of the household of faith." Barr went on to say:

> The minister as pastoral director bears this particular responsibility to those who are of the household of faith and must obey this particular charge. His complaints about the stiff-necked people in his care and the ineffectiveness of his parish in the world are suspect until he has stretched with earnest prayer every gift with which he has been endowed of intellect and imagination and love and physical health to stir his parish to exercise its ministry to the whole world. The minister bears primary responsibility to hold his own being open to and as a channel for the renewing activity of the Creator of the church, to provide the first instance of openness in the church "to the judging and renewing activity of the living God made known in Jesus Christ," an openness which Robert McAfee Brown claims to mark the spirit of Protestantism.[24]

Alvin Toffler has coined the uniquely potent phrase "future shock" to describe "the shattering stress and disorientation that we induce in individuals by subjecting them to too much change in too short a time."[25] We live with a sense of despair and anxiety over massive social issues as new norms and behavior patterns replace traditional values and institutions. A feature article in a recent issue of the *New York Times Magazine* proclaims that "The Family is Out of Fashion."[26] An American president whose political success was based on an uncompromising opposition to communism becomes unexpectedly the chief proponent of *entente cordiale* with the People's Republic of China. What was science fiction only a decade ago becomes for many only a routine event, as the ninth and tenth men stepped on the surface of the moon in the spring of 1972.

The contemporary American pastor is thus faced with unprecedented opportunity and peril. The opportunity lies in the fact that the residentially based, nuclear-family oriented church is peerless among alternative social organizations to minister to the privatized sector of our lives, providing comfort and assurance at a time when our very survival is problematic. The peril of the ministry lies in the temptation to ignore or make peripheral the more impersonal and public dimensions of our parishioners' lives, making religion trivial and a means of escape and social irresponsibility. The peril is real, for the minister is well trained for his ministry to individuals; he needs a new style of theological education to enable him "to cope with the crunch" in these times of escalating social problems.

Elements of a New Style of Education

The elements of this new style of theological education are beginning to emerge in various places. Some of it has certainly been reflected in the changing style of seminary education itself. Long established theological schools are increasingly committed to programs in which students are brought face to face with the concrete world, testing and refining their theological learnings through involvement and action.

In January, 1972, one of the seminaries in this study, located in Hartford, announced that it would drop all of its traditional degree programs and become a new educational support facility for men already in the ministry. According to a news release, the seminary would arrange, on a contract basis, to have courses taught in the clergyman's own community, on a short or long term basis according to the need. Other courses would be arranged for groups of ministers on a regional basis, and faculty will be recruited from both the seminary and from among outside specialists as the need arises.[27]

The change announced for the Hartford Seminary will not take place until the spring of 1973. Among the more striking innovations which have already occurred in the training of ministers is the emergence of action training centers, which have provided internships for seminarians and continuing educational opportunities for pastors. Twenty-one such centers from Los Angeles to New York, and including Canada and Puerto Rico, have formed The Action Training Coalition. This Coalition is responsible for establishing and maintaining high standards for training, procuring funds, and developing common strategies for social change. The goals of these centers are suggested by the following statement of the "training objectives of ATC member agencies":

> Member agencies of ATC offer engagement/reflection action training to enable groups and individuals in socity to effect institutional and community change for humanization and justice. Trainees are sensitized to the problems of the metropolis and trained in such skills as community organization, group process, community analysis, planning, organizational development, issue analysis, and problem solving. In addition, most ATC agencies offer a variety of specialized training programs such as models for dealing with racism, renewal and internal change of the church, urban studies and internships for seminaries, and value systems confrontations.[28]

The new style of theological education will require more than the traditional competence in Biblical, historical, and theological studies. We have already suggested that the minister's authority as a social reformer must become functionally specific to his profession, and this means that he must acquire technical competence as the basis of his leadership.

What is called for is a style of professional education in which the minister is trained for dual competencies or as a multi-specialist. If, in addition to mastering the traditional theological fields of knowledge, he is trained in a second field —as an economist, criminologist, political scientist, sociologist, or whatever—his leadership as a moral leader will have greater authority because it will be based on technical competence.

Obviously not every minister can expect to achieve the same level of technical competence in his secondary field that he has achieved in his primary field. What he can achieve, however, is functional competence in the most critical areas related to the minister's job. In the past he has done this well in the field of pastoral counseling by gaining functional competence in psychology without becoming a psychologist. The same kind of technical competence ought to support the minister in his role as a leader of social reform.

The need for developing dual competencies is not unique to the minister's profession. Alvin Toffler's observations about our future speak directly to the point:

> Despite much loose talk about the need for "generalists," there is little evidence that the technology of tomorrow can be run without armies of highly trained specialists. We are rapidly changing the types of expertise needed. We are demanding more "multi-specialists" (men who know one field deeply, but who can cross over into another as well) rather than rigid, "mono-specialists." But we shall continue to need and breed ever more refined work specialists as the technical base of society increases in complexity. . . .[29]

The training of ministers to become "multi-specialists" is best pursued in professional schools related to universities, for only in such settings are the disciplines of other fields available. The most effective clinical training for ministers is more likely to take place where seminaries have close cooperative arrangements with university psychology departments and medical institutions.

Some of the pain and frustration now being felt by "mono-specialist" ministers might well be diffused if the minister had the competence and ability to "cross over" into another field if he desired to do so. As a multi-specialist, his ministry might be more effective than otherwise because he would know that he continues to be a minister by choice rather than because he is trapped in his profession and has nowhere else to go.

What is required is a style of professional education that is a process, rather than a prescribed curriculum of discrete subject matter. The goal of the minister's study of sociology, for example, is to enable him to think sociologically about his congregation and community, to put informed insight into the theological and Biblical norms which are the foundations of his preaching and pastoral care.

Since no minister can hope to develop technical competence in all fields relevant to his ministry, the new style of education and ministry must be reciprocal. Reciprocity means that many kinds of technical competencies will be available in an association of ministers, and that ministers will be able to call on one another for specialized leadership to meet specific problems and issues. For local congregations, pulpit exchanges will take on an entirely different function and meaning. They will become more frequent and more specialized in purpose, for they become occasions when the congregation is called to grapple with specific issues under the guidance of a guest minister.

To change the style of the minister's education without also changing the institutional context of his professional activities is self-defeating. Undoubtedly the residentially based parish church will continue in the years ahead. It has been particularly functional for an industrial society that was bureaucratically organized, where areas of skill and knowledge were compartmentalized, and when social and economic goals were somewhat clearly discernible.

But what is the shape of the church and the style of its ministry to be in what Toffler calls the "super industrial" age, in which transience, novelty, and diversity are the chief characteristics? The survival of the churches in the past resulted in no small measure from their ability to devise new forms to meet new situations. The revival meeting and circuit rider were social inventions of the church uniquely suited to the American frontier; today's campus ministries and church-sponsored community organizations speak to important sub-cultures of our society. When established institutions become dysfunctional, new social forms emerge. American religious groups are experiencing a plethora of committees, caucuses, task forces, and movements, each addressing itself to specific areas of reform and renewal.

The residentially based parish church can no longer be considered the normative form of church organization; graduates of our theological seminaries must be given alternative church structures in which they can follow their calling. Congregations oriented to political action based on theological reflection, Biblical study, and worship may be one such alternative. Occupation, rather than the family, may well be the organizing principle for another form of ministry. An increasingly leisure-oriented society calls for yet a different institutional structure which can be differentiated from the residentially based parish church. A "new" church to be established in a community may take the form of a bookstore or reading room, a coffee house or day care center, and the minister will be called to serve his parishioners as preacher, teacher, pastor, priest, and prophet in a new setting.

The emerging new style of theological education, in short, must train men capable of inventing new forms of the church for the personal and social needs of parishioners who are not yet born, and for a society whose social and cultural characteristics we have yet to perceive.

Appendix: A Methodological Note

This methodological note is addressed to readers who are interested in the technical aspects of the research on which this volume is based.

During the academic year 1966–1967, Professor Paul M. Harrison of The Pennsylvania State University was engaged by the United Church of Christ to direct a special study for its newly formed Study Commission on Theological Education. During the course of that investigation he visited each of the thirteen seminaries affiliated with the denomination, interviewed its administrators and many of its faculty and students. In addition, he analyzed the curricula and published documents of these institutions and presented his findings in a report to the Study Commission in the spring of 1967. During this period I served as his consultant in my capacity as the research director of the United Church Board for Homeland Ministries, one of the major instrumentalities of the denomination.

Early in 1967 we decided to enlarge the scope of the research by designing a survey of pastors and seminary students to test some of the observations beginning to emerge from the interviews and the seminary publications. We prepared a questionnaire that included items relating to the respondent's educational background, his seminary experience, his conception of the purpose of the church and the work of the minister, his attitude on contemporary social issues, and general informational matters. Some of the questions in the questionnaire were taken from another questionnaire which had recently been used in a survey of a sample of parishioners in the United Church of Christ. Our intention here was to compare the attitudes of clergymen and the laity toward issues relating to church and society.

Since our primary interest was in the training of ministers, we selected as our research population all persons ordained by the United Church of Christ during a five-year period preceding the survey (1962–1966) and a 25 per cent sample of all ministers who were ordained during the previous decade (1952–1961). We arbitrarily limited our population of clergymen to this fifteen-year period because we felt that recollections about one's seminary experience may become less accurate as one grows older.

The names and addresses of our clergy population were drawn from the yearbooks of the United Church of Christ. Of the 1,653 ordainees and ministers available in the research universe as defined, 1,191 ministers returned usable questionnaires. The Post Office returned 48 envelopes because they were undeliverable for one reason or another; 15 persons returned their questionnaires to us without answering them. Our over-all response rate was 77.1 per cent of the available clergy universe.

To achieve this rate of response, we sent the questionnaire with a covering letter and postage-paid return envelope by first class mail, asking the recipient's cooperation to help the denomination to plan more effectively for the future education of its ministers. The questionnaires were to be returned to The Pennsylvania State University, where the research was being conducted. A postcard addressed to the research office of the denomination in New York City was also included in the first mailing. The purpose of this card was to let us know that the individual had returned his questionnaire to the University so that a follow-up would not be required.

About two weeks after the first mailing, a second questionnaire with a covering letter and return envelope was mailed to all ministers who had not returned a postcard. Approximately 20 per cent of our returns came as a result of this second mailing.

The questionnaire was designed in such a way that the respondent's identity would remain anonymous. We believe that our unusually high return rate for this group was due, not only to the self-interest of the clergymen in the purposes of the survey, but to the effort we made to assure the confidentiality of their answers.

Our research population also included students who were enrolled in the thirteen theological seminaries affiliated with the United Church of Christ. We were far less successful in gaining the full cooperation of this group. A major reason is that 7 of the 13 schools are interdenominational, and many students undoubtedly failed to respond because they were members of other denominations. Furthermore, since many of the students lived in seminary housing units, we asked administrators in each seminary to distribute the questionnaires for us. We also asked them, after two weeks, to make several general announcements to their student bodies reminding them to return the questionnaires. As in the case of the ministers, the questionnaires were to be mailed to the University's research office. We did not include the postcard to follow up on nonresponding students.

The seminaries reported a total of 2,771 students to whom questionnaires could be sent. The return rate varied from 36 per cent for Union Theological Seminary (which had the largest enrollment) to 86 per cent for the Chicago Theological Seminary. The 1,283 usable questionnaires received from seminarians accounted for an over-all return rate of 46.3 per cent. Since our cut-off date for processing questionnaires occurred after the end of the school year, we were unable to follow up on the nonresponding students in any systematic way.

The seminarians' return rate varied for the three groups of seminaries in the survey. We achieved the highest return rate of 62 per cent from the former Congregational Christian seminaries. Fifty-four per cent of the students enrolled in former Evangelical and Reformed schools returned information, while returns from students in the interdenominational schools accounted for 40 per cent of that group.

The questions were identical for pastors and seminarians. Most of the questions required forced option responses; others required scaled responses indicating degrees of agreement or importance. The responses were pre-coded to facilitate automatic tabulation.

In the study, we have used the chi-square test of significance where appropriate. While we have considered the 5 per cent level of significance to be the criterion of acceptance, most of the tables included in this volume are significant at the .001 level.

Finally, the data concerning the laity of the denomination are drawn from an earlier volume, *The Fragmented Layman: An Empirical Study of Lay Attitudes,* which I co-authored with Thomas C. Campbell and which was published by Pilgrim Press in 1970. Details concerning the research design for that study will be found in that volume.

The major portion of the funding for this research was provided by the United Church Board for Homeland Ministries through its Division of Higher Education and the American Missionary Association. Additional funds were also provided by the Central Research Fund of the College of Liberal Arts of The Pennsylvania State University.

Notes

Preface

1. Paul M. Harrison, "Theological Education and the United Church of Christ," mimeographed (April 15, 1967), p. ii.
2. Paul M. Harrison, *Authority and Power in the Free Church Tradition: A Social Case Study of the American Baptist Convention* (Princeton: Princeton University Press, 1959).
3. Thomas C. Campbell and Yoshio Fukuyama, *The Fragmented Layman: An Empirical Study of Lay Attitudes* (Boston and Philadelphia: Pilgrim Press, 1970).
4. This classification of the thirteen seminaries affiliated with the United Church of Christ is also followed by the American Association of Theological Schools in the most recent *Directory* of member institutions (1971).

Chapter 1

1. H. Richard Niebuhr, *The Purpose of the Church and its Ministry* (New York: Harper and Bros., 1956), p. 50.
2. W. A. Brown and Mark A. May, *The Education of American Ministers,* 4 vols. (New York: Institute for Social and Religious Research, 1934).
3. James D. Glasse, *Profession: Minister* (Nashville: Abingdon Press, 1968), p. 13.
4. "Drought Hits the Halls of Divinity," *The Christian Century,* Vol. 88, No. 4 (January 27, 1971), p. 91.
5. Browne Barr, "Lineaments of Seminary Renewal," *The Christian Century,* Vol. 88, No. 4 (January 27, 1971), p. 97.
6. For an elaboration of the technical aspects of the research design for this study, see the Methodological Note in the Appendix.
7. Ardis Whitman, "The View from the Pulpit," *McCall's* (February, 1968), p. 83.

8. Ibid., p. 145.
9. Ibid.
10. Campbell and Fukuyama, *The Fragmented Layman.*
11. Samuel W. Blizzard, "The Minister's Dilemma," *The Christian Century,* Vol. 73, No. 17 (April 25, 1956), pp. 508–510.
12. James M. Gustafson, "The Clergy in the United States," *Daedalus,* Vol. 92, No. 4 (Fall, 1963), p. 725.
13. Ibid.
14. Ibid.
15. Wilhelm Pauck, "The Ministry in the Time of the Continental Reformation," in H. Richard Niebuhr and Daniel D. Williams, eds., *The Ministry in Historical Perspectives* (New York: Harper and Bros., 1956), pp. 131–132.
16. Winthrop S. Hudson, "The Ministry in the Puritan Age," in Niebuhr and Williams, pp. 183–184.

Chapter 2

1. Brown and May, *Education of American Ministers,* Vol. 2, p. 33.
2. Richard A. La Piere, *Theory of Social Control* (New York: McGraw-Hill, 1954), p. 409.
3. Robert W. Hodge, Paul M. Siegel, and Peter H. Rossi, "Occupational Prestige in the United States, 1925–63," *American Journal of Sociology,* Vol. 70, No. 3 (November, 1964), pp. 286–302.
4. Alex Inkeles and Peter H. Rossi, "National Comparisons of Occupational Prestige," *American Journal of Sociology,* Vol. 61, No. 4 (January, 1956), pp. 329–339.
5. U.S. Census of Population, 1960. PC(2)-7A, *Occupational Characteristics* (Washington, D.C.: U.S. Government Printing Office, 1963).
6. James M. Gustafson, "Clergy," p. 741.
7. Ibid., p. 742.
8. Truman B. Douglass, "The Job the Protestants Shirk," *Harper's* (November, 1958), pp. 45–49.
9. Keith R. Bridston and Dwight W. Culver, *Pre-Seminary Education* (Minneapolis: Augsburg Publishing House, 1965), p. 37.
10. Ibid.
11. Pauck, "Continental Reformation," p. 144.
12. See Note 10, above.

13. Arthur J. Vidich and Joseph Bensman, *Small Town in Mass Society* (Princeton: Princeton University Press, 1958), Chapter 2.
14. Campbell and Fukuyama, *The Fragmented Layman,* pp. 226–227.
15. Browne Barr, *Parish Back Talk: The Lyman Beecher Lectures, 1963* (New York and Nashville: Abingdon Press, 1964).

Chapter 3

1. Paul M. Harrison, "Theological Education and the United Church of Christ," p. 42.
2. See Table 1–5.
3. James M. Gustafson, *Treasure in Earthen Vessels* (New York: Harper and Bros., 1961), p. 61.

Chapter 4

1. Kenneth Underwood, *The Church, The University, and Social Policy* (Middletown, Conn.: Wesleyan University Press, 1969), Vol. 1, p. 453.
2. Ibid., Chapter 21.
3. Ibid., p. 431.
4. James E. Dittes, *Minister on the Spot* (Philadelphia: Pilgrim Press, 1970), p. 102.
5. Ordway Tead, *The Art of Administration* (New York: McGraw-Hill, 1951), p. 100.
6. Underwood, *Church, University, and Social Policy,* p. 473.
7. Dittes, *Minister,* p. 111.
8. Tead, *Administration,* p. 4.
9. Ibid., p. 13.
10. Ibid., p. 17.
11. Dittes, *Minister,* pp. 113–114.
12. Francis X. Pirazzini, "Loveletter to the Seminaries," *The Christian Ministry,* Vol. 3, No. 2 (March, 1972), p. 32.
13. Campbell and Fukuyama, *The Fragmented Layman,* p. 64.
14. Gibson Winter, *The Suburban Captivity of the Churches* (Garden City: Doubleday & Co., 1961), pp. 131–140.
15. Ibid., p. 105.
16. Ibid., p. 131.

17. Gerald J. Jud, Edgar W. Mills, and Genevieve W. Burch, *Ex-Pastors: Why Men Leave the Parish Ministry* (Philadelphia: Pilgrim Press, 1970), p. 180.
18. D. Keith Mano, "Letter from an Angry Episcopalian," *New York Magazine* (May 10, 1971).
19. Reinhold Niebuhr, *Moral Man and Immoral Society* (New York: Scribners, 1932).

Chapter 5

1. Pierre Berton, *The Comfortable Pew* (Toronto: McClelland & Stewart, 1965), pp. 95–96.
2. Charles Y. Glock, Benjamin B. Ringer, and Earl R. Babbie, *To Comfort and to Challenge* (Berkeley: University of California Press, 1967), pp. 107–108.
3. Max Weber, *The Sociology of Religion* (Boston: Beacon Press, 1962), p. 69.
4. Ernst Troeltsch, *The Social Teaching of the Christian Churches* (New York: Macmillan, 1949), Vol. 1, pp. 331–354.
5. Martin Marty, *The New Shape of American Religion* (New York: Harper and Bros., 1959); Peter L. Berger, *The Noise of Solemn Assemblies* (Garden City: Doubleday & Co., 1961); Harvey Cox, *The Secular City* (New York: Macmillan, 1965).
6. Jeffrey K. Hadden, *The Gathering Storm in the Churches* (Garden City: Doubleday-Anchor, 1970), pp. 5–6, 239.
7. Ibid., pp. 250–251.
8. Ibid., p. 251.
9. Ibid., pp. 180–181.
10. The statistical data for the attitudes of laymen in the United Church of Christ reported in this volume are taken from Campbell and Fukuyama, *The Fragmented Layman.*
11. For representative names used in this question to identify each political label, see Table 5–5.

Chapter 6

1. Charles Y. Glock, "The Sociology of Religion," in Robert K. Merton, Leonard Broom, and Leonard S. Cottrell, Jr., eds., *Sociology To-*

day: Problems and Prospects (New York: Basic Books, 1959), p. 162.

2. H. Richard Niebuhr, *The Social Sources of Denominationalism* (New York: Henry Holt & Co., 1929).
3. See Page Smith, *As a City Upon a Hill* (New York: Knopf, 1966), esp. pp. 37–54.
4. For a history of Congregationalism see Gaius Glenn Atkins and Frederick L. Fagley, *History of American Congregationalism* (Boston: Pilgrim Press, 1942); for a history of the American Missionary Association, see Fred L. Brownlee, *New Day Ascending* (Boston: Pilgrim Press, 1946).
5. Frank A. Kostyu, "A History of the United Church," pamphlet (Division of Publication, United Church Board for Homeland Ministries, n.d.), p. 32.
6. Yoshio Fukuyama, "Churches and Church Membership in the United States," mimeographed (Board of Home Missions of the Congregational and Christian Churches, January 29, 1960).
7. "Historical Sketches of the Congregational Christian Churches and the Evangelical and Reformed Church," pamphlet (published jointly by the General Council of the Congregational Christian Churches and the General Council of the Evangelical and Reformed Church, 1955).
8. For an extensive bibliographic essay, see David O. Moberg, "Social Class and the Churches," in *Information Service*, Vol. 37, No. 12 (June 14, 1958), pp. 6–8.
9. An example of this appears in Herbert Schneider, *Religion in 20th Century America* (Cambridge: Harvard University Press, 1952), Appendix, p. 228. Schneider ranks religious groups in the following order: Christian Scientist, Episcopal, Congregational, Presbyterian, Jewish, Reformed, Methodist, Lutheran, Christian, Protestant (small bodies), Roman Catholic, Baptist, and Mormon. See also N. J. Demerath III, *Social Class in American Protestantism* (Chicago: Rand McNally, 1965).
10. This is the thesis argued by Robert Lee in *The Social Sources of Church Unity* (New York: Abingdon Press, 1960).
11. Harrison, "Theological Education," p. 56.

Chapter 7

1. Wilbert E. Moore, *The Professions: Roles and Rules* (New York: Russell Sage Foundation, 1970), p. 10.

2. W. J. Reader, *Professional Men: The Rise of the Professional Classes in Nineteenth-Century England* (London: Weidenfeld and Nicolson, 1966).
3. Daniel H. Calhoun, *Professional Lives in America* (Cambridge: Harvard University Press, 1965).
4. Moore, *The Professions,* pp. 245–301.
5. Amitai Etzioni, ed., *The Semi-Professions and their Organization: Teachers, Nurses and Social Workers* (New York: Free Press, 1969).
6. J. Anthony Lukas, "Historians' Conference: The Radical Need for Jobs," *The New York Times Magazine* (March 12, 1972), p. 39.
7. Talcott Parsons, *Essays in Sociological Theory Pure and Applied* (Glencoe: Free Press, 1949), p. 185, 198–199.
8. Ibid., p. 186.
9. Ernest Q. Campbell and Thomas F. Pettigrew, "Racial and Moral Crisis: The Role of Little Rock Ministers," *American Journal of Sociology,* Vol. 64, No. 5 (March, 1959), pp. 509–516.
10. Phillip E. Hammond, *The Campus Clergyman* (New York: Basic Books, 1966).
11. Parsons, *Essays in Sociological Theory,* p. 189.
12. Ibid., p. 193.
13. Arthur J. Vidich and Joseph Bensman, *Small Town in Mass Society* (Princeton: Princeton University Press, 1968), pp. 241 ff.
14. Campbell and Pettigrew, "Racial and Moral Crisis," p. 509.
15. Bernard Barber, "Some Problems in the Sociology of Professions," *Daedalus,* Vol. 92, No. 4 (Fall, 1963), p. 674.
16. Ibid.
17. Ibid., pp. 674–675.
18. Jud et al., *Ex-Pastors,* p. 49.
19. Max Weber, *The Theory of Social and Economic Organization* (New York: Oxford University Press, 1947), Chapter 1.
20. Harold R. Fray, Jr., *The Pain and Joy of Ministry* (Manuscript of a volume to be published by Pilgrim Press, Philadelphia).
21. Ibid., p. 27c.
22. Ibid., p. 4.
23. Ibid., p. 6.
24. Browne Barr, *Parish Back Talk: The Lyman Beecher Lectures, 1963* (New York and Nashville: Abindgon Press, 1964), p. 68.
25. Alvin Toffler, *Future Shock* (New York: Random House, 1970), p. 2.
26. Ann Richardson Roiphe, "The Family is Out of Fashion," *The New York Times Magazine* (August 15, 1971), pp. 10 ff.

27. *The New York Times* (January 31, 1972): *United Church Herald* (April, 1972), pp. 8–9.
28. "Action Training Coalition Directory 1970."
29. Toffler, *Future Shock,* p. 288.

Index